We Are Sew Powerful

Jason & Cinnamon Miles

We Are Sew Powerful

*How A Global Community Of Seamstresses Is
Changing Zambia One Girl At A Time*

Jason G. Miles & Cinnamon Miles

ISBN 978-0-692-79339-8

Published in the United States by Sew Powerful Press

Sew Powerful Press
218 E. Main Street
Auburn, WA 98002

About the Authors

Jason G. Miles is the co-founder of Liberty Jane® and Sew Powerful. He holds a graduate degree in Business Administration with an emphasis in International non-profit management, as well as undergraduate degrees in both Organizational Management and Biblical Studies.

Before joining Liberty Jane Clothing and Sew Powerful full-time he served as the Senior Vice President of Advancement at Northwest University. Prior to that he served as an Executive Director at World Vision where he spent sixteen years in both Human Resources and fundraising.

Cinnamon Miles is the co-founder and lead designer at Liberty Jane® and Sew Powerful. She manages the company's premiere web property, www.pixiefaire.com, the world's largest doll clothes pattern marketplace with over 1.5 million patterns downloaded. Cinnamon is also the bestselling author of *The Idiot's Guide: Sewing* published with DK Publishing.

Cinnamon's international experience includes serving with Youth With A Mission in Eastern Europe, and on numerous short-term missions to places such as Latvia, Mexico City, Romania, and Zambia.

Table of Contents

Foreword

By Jason

This book is about a sewing program in a very unlikely place—Ngombe Compound in Lusaka, Zambia. Ngombe is pronounced "Nom-Bay." It is one of the most crowded and desperate urban slums in Zambia.

Our goal in Ngombe is to work with the moms in a respectful and collaborative way so that they achieve a local impact that can truly transform their local school, neighborhood—and one day, all of Zambia.

At the same time, we want the moms in the program to make a personal income that lifts them from poverty based on their hard work. We call what we've created a "sewing cooperative," because they share a location, machines, leadership, and a mission.

Scaling up the production of high-quality products to address a real problem is very important to us. We are capitalists at heart. We want customers to pay for things whenever possible, and we want a positive local economic impact from our work.

We've come to realize the strength and value of creating donor involvement methods that give people from around the world a meaningful way to support these goals with their time, talent, and treasure.

But we also believe charity can do harm. If we give in the wrong way, we destroy the motivation, enthusiasm, and hustle that can frequently accompany the pursuit of a noble cause. And the moms of Ngombe have a noble cause. Their intensity of pursuit to achieve success for their children is a special attribute, and we want to add fuel to that fire, support it, and not quench it.

Although I've written most of the chapters in this book from my voice, this is really a group project with Cinnamon helping me shape the content. Her wisdom, business insight, and incredible talent have made Sew Powerful, and this book, possible.

When we began writing, we also invited people to submit their stories. We were amazed at what we received, so we've added an entire section filled with those stories. We hope they inspire you as much as they did us.

You'll also find chapters written from our family, board members, friends, and program partners. We owe them a huge debt of gratitude for their hard work on this book. We'd also like to thank Deana Guardado for her wonderful help editing the book.

To make your experience more engaging we set up a companion webpage with lots of pictures. You can see it at:

http://www.sewpowerful.org/book

As a group, we are working hard to build something that is unique and effective. We have no interest in charity handouts that damage or destroy the economic opportunities within poor communities. Instead, we want the full impact of a vibrant local sewing cooperative that is producing meaningful products to empower local educational achievement and health goals, backed by an enthusiastic global community of co-workers.

I hope this book opens a whole new world to you—a world where we don't just give money to the poor, but instead we work right alongside them, to accomplish common goals that they define and we support. Together we can combat extreme poverty with sewing. Together we are Sew Powerful.

Foreword

Thank you again for taking the time to learn more about the mission and purpose of Sew Powerful. If you enjoy this book, then do us a huge favor—hand it to a friend and ask them to read it too.

Jason Miles & Cinnamon Miles
September 1, 2016
Auburn, Washington

PART ONE

The Sew Powerful Story

"Here's to the crazy ones, the misfits, the rebels, the troublemakers, the round pegs in the square holes... The ones who see things differently— they're not fond of rules... You can quote them, disagree with them, glorify or vilify them, but the only thing you can't do is ignore them because they change things... They push the human race forward, and while some may see them as the crazy ones, we see genius, because the ones who are crazy enough to think that they can change the world, are the ones who do."

—Apple

Ngombe Compound

By Jason

A s an employee for World Vision, I had the privilege of leading lots of trips to Africa and other places around the world, from Honduras to Romania. I've visited dozens of communities and schools. I've dug latrines for widows in Honduras, held Vacation Bible School in the slums of Mexico City, and visited people in Hospitals in Ukraine. But in March 2009, I visited a very special group in Zambia.

That day something inside me snapped. I guess you could say I fell in love with the place, the people, and the problems. There is no better way to describe it. I wasn't heart-broken—I was the opposite of that—I was in love. For some reason, I couldn't leave that day emotionally. I guess you could call it an unstoppable enthusiasm for it. That day I adopted 475 kids in my heart and mind.

I was leading a group from Menlo Park Presbyterian Church. We had the privilege of traveling to Zambia to meet HIV/AIDS Caregivers, walk from house to house with them, meet their clients, and learn about their work as the front-line soldiers in the war against HIV/AIDS.

Entering Ngombe Compound

The place we were going to visit that day was a community school. In Zambia, you generally have three types of schools: government, private, and community. Private schools are similar to what we'd be familiar with in the west, a more affluent option. The community schools are generally thought of as the worst, since moms and volunteers primarily run them and there is no government funding or support.

We really shouldn't have even been there that day at all.

It was on a day when we didn't have any specific program-related visits to do, because something had gotten rearranged.

So Kristin, our World Vision Zambia office host, improvised a bit, and asked if we wanted to go and see a distribution of blankets at a community school.

She said, *"It's in Ngombe Compound, which is one of the poorest urban slums in Lusaka."* The term compound is used like we use the term neighborhood. So across the city there were numerous compounds, and Ngombe had a reputation for being a very challenging place.

We all agreed we wanted to go. But she warned us, *"Ngombe is like nothing you've ever seen before."*

Ngombe is not far from the Parliament building in the Capital City of Lusaka. It has somewhere between 130,000 and 150,000 people living in it. Half the residents are under the age of fifteen, because many of the adults have died from AIDS, tuberculosis, or malaria.

Today it has one paved road that runs through it, but at the time there weren't any. There is no garbage system, so there are several ravines that serve as community garbage dumps. Today it has several community water taps, but not water in each home.

Many of the adults that live in Ngombe work outside the community as security guards, gardeners, and housemaids. They walk out to the main road early in the morning and then make their way to their job. The average household income in Zambia is $113 per month, so even paying for public transportation is hard.

To get water in Ngombe, you have to carry your can, walk to the community tap, and pay the attendant to get water. Ngombe's not a place built for cars or delivery trucks, but you'll frequently find them there trying to navigate the dirt roads and massive potholes. There are small makeshift shops and other types of tiny businesses along the main roads.

Entering Ngombe is visually overwhelming. There are always thousands of people walking in every direction, most of them children. Babies and toddlers are wandering barefoot everywhere.

The Needs Care School

Our destination that day was a partially completed church building. It was fairly large—or at least, it was going to be when it was completed. The school was using the church while it was under construction.

A local woman named Esther had started the school with a group of likeminded moms in 2003. They had started with just under one hundred kids; but by the time we visited them in 2009, they had four hundred and seventy-five children.

The school was started because none of the children in the community could afford to attend the government school, which requires various small fees, the cost of uniforms, and other expenses, which are impossible for parents or guardians to pay. The moms of the community—particularly Esther—were desperate to do something to educate the children.

The school was named the Needs Care School. What a funny name—but it was fairly descriptive. As we arrived, Esther greeted us enthusiastically, welcomed us to the school, and walked us into the building. It was a huge, dusty, cavernous space. The block walls had gaps that let light into the otherwise dark interior of the building. Some were in the shape of the cross; it made the visual effect of the space oddly interesting.

We sat down and the children sang and danced for us. We were the guests of honor and they had prepared for our visit. They had never had a group of fifteen "muzungus," the African term for white people, visit before. Esther asked me to greet the children and introduce our group. Then to my surprise, she asked me to dance for the children. I'd never been asked to do that before! So I did my best, danced as they sang, and we laughed the whole way through.

After the singing, Esther began sharing more about the school. They offered grades one through seven. Each class would huddle in a different corner of the church. It was noisy, dusty, and chaotic, but somehow magical.

Figure 1.1 *Meeting Esther at Needs Care in 2009*

The Children Of Ngombe

Esther explained that almost half of the children were HIV positive. Suddenly the mood of our group sank as we began to realize the gravity of the situation.

She said the largest struggle they face is the lack of food in the community. Getting the children to pay attention in class when they haven't eaten is hard. Esther explained how the children come in the morning, and at every break the youngest ones say, "I'm hungry," The third and fourth graders politely ask if they can have a little bit of food so their stomachs don't make noises. The sixth and seventh grade children know we don't have any food, so they stop asking.

She went on to share that two-thirds of the children have lost both parents, usually due to AIDS, Tuberculosis, or Malaria, and many of the rest had lost one parent.

One of the women from our group asked, *"Do the orphans all sleep here at night?"*

Esther explained that in Africa, they don't use the word "orphan," because they believe they are children of the community. They sleep in the homes of the aunties, grandmas, cousins, or other distant relatives. In the case of a family having an older sibling that is a teenager, that child becomes the head of the household and takes responsibility for the young brothers and sisters.

Figure 1.2 *Meeting the children of Ngombe*

The HIV/AIDS Crisis

Like many Southern African nations, the HIV/AIDS crisis devastated the country and really impacted Ngombe in particular. If there was a place completely torn apart by HIV/AIDS, it was Ngombe Compound. If you're not familiar with the history of the African spread of HIV/AIDS, then it's worth a short explanation. If you don't understand it correctly, you won't understand the situation for the children in Ngombe, Needs Care, or Sew Powerful.

Epidemiologists believe the origin of the disease was the Democratic Republic of Congo, which borders Zambia to the north.

Unlike in the United States, in the Southern African nations, HIV/AIDS was spread as a heterosexual disease. Southern African countries include Angola, Botswana, Lesotho, Malawi, Mozambique, Namibia, Southern Africa, Swaziland, Zambia, and Zimbabwe. In the 1970s and 1980s HIV/AIDS was making its way throughout Southern Africa. Truckers that frequented prostitutes and then drove on to other destinations became one group of unwitting transmitters.

So while medical experts in the west were trying to figure out what HIV/AIDS was, how to diagnose it, and treat it, in Southern Africa, it was being spread very quickly through the population. Since HIV doesn't have any immediate signs or signals when initially contracted, people who felt healthy didn't know they were spreading it.

Because the situation in Southern Africa is very different than in the United States, it's hard for us in the west to understand how it was able to kill 35 million people, and how another 36 million are living with it worldwide.

In Zambia, according to the UN, it's estimated that almost 13% percent of the population has HIV. That number has fallen significantly because of the death of so many people. But the percentages increase substantially when you look at 15–49 year olds, and then skyrockets when you enter an urban slum like Ngombe. Many children are HIV Positive as well.

Why HIV Spread So Far

The reason HIV/AIDS was particularly devastating was because of a lack of knowledge about the disease, poor healthcare infrastructure, and a set of cultural and traditional practices that created a domino effect.

There was a lack of knowledge because the population has a very high rate of illiteracy, particularly in places like Ngombe. So a lot of the education about HIV/AIDS in the early years was from rumor, gossip, and mass media. All kinds of incorrect information spread about the disease. There were rumors and legends about how to prevent it, and even how to cure it. The myth that sex with a virgin cures AIDS was the most devastating.

There was, and still is, poor healthcare infrastructure. But a lot has changed in the last ten years. There are clinics that have educated nurses and doctors, and HIV tests are now commonly available. Anti-Retroviral Therapy drugs that delay the onset of full-blown AIDS are also distributed to those who need them. But people still avoid being tested for a variety of reasons.

The traditional practices in Zambia are the most uncommon to us in the west, so they're the hardest to understand. But once you learn about them, you can begin to grasp how they impacted the country.

Before we judge their traditional practices, we should remember we have our own in our countries. We just grow familiar with them. Zambians would be surprised to learn that over 50% of marriages in the United States end in divorce.

The Zambian practice most commonly associated with the spread of HIV is a practice known as "Widow Cleansing." In this practice, when a man dies, his brother inherits the widowed wife and they are expected to sleep together, or bad luck will follow their households. You can imagine how, when husbands are dying of HIV/AIDS, how quickly that practice transmits HIV. Government leaders are working to end this practice and educate families about the spread of HIV.

There are other factors that fueled HIV transmission including mother-to-child transmission, exposure to blood, polygamy, and marriages of very young girls to older HIV Positive men out of desperation.

Sadly, some American Christians have been quick to chalk all of this up to immorality. But I don't think that's justified. I've visited homes with HIV/AIDS caregivers throughout Southern Africa and met their patients. I've heard their stories and prayed with them.

I can promise you, Americans don't have any moral high ground compared to the people of Southern Africa. If the U.S. healthcare system and illiteracy rates matched those in Zambia, then I believe the

U.S. HIV rate would match theirs too. I'd imagine the same goes for other western nations. These could be our children, our nieces, our grandchildren. It could be our neighborhood.

American Christians also assume that Zambians aren't Christians, but that is not accurate. According to a census done in 2000, the population of Zambia is 87% Christian, a much higher percentage than the United States. Other Southern African nations have very high percentages of Christians as well. To see the situation correctly we need to challenge our own biases and assumptions.

Esther then explained that with World Vision's help, they had trained 90 HIV/AIDS caregivers. The caregivers were led by a gracious older man. He and about a dozen of the caregivers were there to greet us. He explained a bit about the program, and we were incredibly impressed with their care for the local community.

The Moms of Ngombe

Our tour moved on, and Esther introduced us to a group of moms. She explained that they were trying to make jewelry and sell it locally to support the school. As you might imagine, trying to sell inexpensive jewelry in a slum in Zambia wasn't too profitable. But the jewelry looked nice, so when we offered to buy everything they had made, they burst into clapping, dancing, and shouts of "Amen!" It was a fun moment.

I wondered why the moms were trying to raise money for the school. It's not that a fundraiser wasn't obviously needed, but I wondered, from their perspective, what were they trying to achieve in terms of their goals and hopes. The situation seemed so overwhelming from where we sat.

As they shared, we felt the heartbeat of those moms for their children in a vibrant way. Their passion for their kids was unstoppable, mesmerizing, and contagious. They wanted them educated at all costs. They had a very simple set of goals.

> ✓ First, they wanted the children to get a good education. They wanted them to learn to read and write.

✓ Second, they hoped to someday have a healthy school lunch to serve so the children were able to concentrate.

✓ Third, they dreamed of having their own school—a nice building with qualified teachers, bathrooms and even a kitchen.

✓ Fourth, they wanted the kids (and the community) physically healthy.

✓ Fifth, they wanted to personally work and make money to support these goals.

The Place People Run From

As I stood in the Needs Care School, I began to wonder why more people weren't helping Esther. I expected that because of the desperation in Ngombe, large Christian International charities would operate their programs there. Maybe they do, but we haven't found them there.

Non-Profits and Christian ministries all have their reasons for not being in Ngombe, and we don't fault them. But it is disheartening to know that amongst the poorest of the poor, you won't find the large American non-profit organizations operating as vibrantly as you might expect. We learned that "Muzungus" were uncommon in Ngombe Compound.

World Vision, the organization I worked for when I first visited Ngombe, didn't have any program locations there. They loved Esther's program, wanted to help, but didn't have any ongoing programs or funding that they could allocate to Ngombe. The reason is fairly pragmatic.

The World Vision funding model is child sponsorship. That model only works in rural villages where the population of children is very stable so that you can take pictures, do check-ups, monitor outcomes, and ensure that the benefits of the program are sustainable. In Ngombe the children come and go too quickly, either by relocation or death.

The World Vision Zambia team does what it can to help Esther within their budget constraints. It includes inviting her team to training, and allocating donations of clothing and related items, like blankets, to Needs Care when they can. But her school is just one of thousands of small community based organizations in a country full of need.

The large churches we've visited in Lusaka don't have programs in Ngombe either. We assume some do, but like churches in the U.S., these large successful churches have their own ministry locations and priorities.

At the time of our visit, Esther had no outside funding to support the school. She had no Zambian government or charity support either. She was on her own, but wasn't going to let finances stop her from delivering education to the kids of the community.

I learned later that even some American missionaries stationed in Zambia avoid Ngombe out of fear, frustration, and futility. Believe it or not, we've even had career American missionaries living in Zambia (for decades) say to us,

> *"We've only gone into Ngombe Compound one time in all these years, and the roads were so bad we couldn't figure out how to turn the car around to leave. But we pass it regularly because it's on the way to a retreat center we like to go eat at."*

Our Calling

Of course I was outraged when I heard the missionaries say those words, but sadly not surprised. Ngombe just doesn't seem to be a place they feel is part of their calling. It's more like a place people run from.

What I mean by a calling is a deep spiritual or emotional feeling that can only be described as a permanent obsession. That day as I stood in the Needs Care School, God put a passion for that place into my heart and mind that I cannot undo.

I'm mentally, emotionally, and financially invested in Ngombe, and I realize that most people aren't. Maybe one day we'll move there; but I feel that for now, we can accomplish more by staying here and serving as donors, fundraisers and cheerleaders for Esther and the moms of Ngombe. It's their ministry, not ours.

Why did that visit to Ngombe impact me so deeply? I'm not entirely sure. But the children were beautiful. The teachers were heroic. Esther was capable and highly respected. Sure, the conditions were horrible, but they were working hard to reach their goals.

I know it might sound odd, but I also took some of the best pictures of my life that day, which was a minor photographic miracle. Going on several previous short-term trips with a professional photographer had helped me prepare, but on this trip I was on my own. My tutor on the prior trips was an incredible professional named Mark Kuroda. Mark is from San Francisco, and has worked with many of the top clothing brands in the world, so I had a great coach.

As I walked into the dark, dusty church, I knew I had a photographic challenge. When I walked out, I had a challenge of a whole different variety.

Our Road to Ngombe

By Jason

A few days later, we had finished up our trip and headed home. I went home and told Cinnamon all about the school, Esther, the children, and their need for support. My pictures helped share the story.

Cinnamon and I had just gone through our own financial trauma, and we certainly didn't feel like we had any extra money to give. I knew it was a huge stretch to even bring up the idea, but I told her I really felt strongly that we needed to figure out a way to personally support Esther. Nervously, after I had explained everything I asked, *"What about $100 a month?"*

She graciously agreed. But then she said, *"How are you even going to get her the money?"* I had no idea. But we started to figure it out.

I got in touch with Esther and let her know what we wanted to do. All I could figure out was to wire her the money through my bank. Unfortunately, they charged me $50 for each wire transfer, so the school only got $50. It was a horrible method of giving, but it was the only thing we could figure out at the time.

Doubling Our Support

We struggled with the bank wire fees for almost a year. Then we found our solution by working with a ministry in Northern California called

"Kids For The Kingdom." Greg Dabel, the founder, was gracious enough to begin covering the banking fees for us, so our $100 could go straight to the school. That small change in the process felt like our first miracle. Greg was a godsend. It doubled our monthly giving. After Greg found out about Esther, he began contributing each month too.

Several years later, the leaders of the church building that Esther was using as the school in Ngombe, told Esther that their church was nearing completion; she was going to have to find a new place for conducting school. She had no idea what she was going to do. Greg organized a trip with a donor; to everyone's shock, the donor paid for the purchase of land and the construction of a new school. The new school was completed in 2013. That donor, although we've never met her and don't even know her name, was another godsend.

Even though Cinnamon and I had gone through our own recent financial trauma and didn't feel like we were in a position to give very much financially to Esther, we felt like it was something we had to do.

Our Toxic Mortgage Mess

Four years before I met Esther, in 2005, after having worked at World Vision for over a decade, we were asked to be the San Francisco Bay Area Directors. The job meant we could be closer to family, so we accepted the job offer and moved our young family to Northern California. Housing was insanely expensive, so we moved to the outskirts of the Bay Area, to the small town of Dixon in Solano County.

Tragically, we decided to use a new mortgage product we had never heard of before called a Neg-Am loan. Before we realized it, we found ourselves in a huge mortgage mess. We were stupid, didn't read the fine print, didn't realize the consequences, and didn't ask enough questions. So while my new job was going well, we were in real trouble financially.

As 2005 turned into 2006, the housing market in Northern California started to fall apart. Because of the terms of our loan, our monthly mortgage payment more than doubled in 2007. We had a lot of sleepless nights.

As 2007 neared, our youngest daughter was preparing to enter Kindergarten. Cinnamon, then, had a few hours in the middle of the day to try to help us solve our financial mess.

Rather than having her try to find a part-time job, we decided to find a way she could make money from home. During 2007 she tried her hand at family photography. We found that the in-person selling, late nights and weekends, and general bad economics of photography, meant that her first venture wasn't going to solve our financial problems.

But that year something else began to happen. Cinnamon started making doll clothes for our daughters. American Girl dolls were popular with the girls and their friends. We stretched financially to buy one of them for our daughter's birthday, and Cinnamon made a set of matching outfits. The moms at the Girl Scout Troop started to ask where those cute clothes came from. Cinnamon would always answer, "*I just made them. It's not hard; I can show you how if you want.*" To which she'd hear back, "*I don't know how to sew.*"

Cinnamon learned to make doll clothes as an eight-year-old, so for her it came naturally. She has an ability to obsess over it to a level that most people don't understand. It's not uncommon for her to spend two or three weeks making one design. Her mom had worked for a Fashion Designer in L.A. as a "cutter," so Cinnamon had both the passion and professional training that made her work very unique.

During the winter of 2007 we listed her first outfits as an auction on eBay. I helped with the listing descriptions. Twenty minutes later, we received an email from a doll collector asking a very specific question about the construction of the item. We were blown away. The item sold for $39, about the same price as a "real" American Girl doll outfit. We found auctions fairly easy to do, and she liked the work-from-home-over-the-Internet nature of the activity.

A plan came together. In February 2008, we formally opened our eBay store with the goal of making $1,000 a month with our new business that we named "Liberty Jane Clothing." It was named after our daughter Liberty, and she and I started doing YouTube contest videos to help spread the word about Cinnamon's designs.

Cinnamon would make the items and photograph them, and I would help with the marketing-related activities. Our auctions started to go for increasingly higher prices, from $39 to $79, to $199, and higher. Our highest auction to date ended at just over $500.

Figure 2.1 *Cinnamon's designs draw a crowd*

Tearful Goodbyes

During both 2008 and 2009 we hit our $1,000 a month goal with our eBay selling; but sadly, the little business wasn't strong enough financially to keep us from losing our house. We knew we had to make a change, and I accepted a job back in Seattle with World Vision.

The low point was in January 2009, standing in our kitchen and telling our kids we were going to move back to Seattle. Our middle daughter hugged me with tears in her eyes and said, *"Dad, you said we would never have to move again."* I was heartsick.

With a lot tears and sad goodbyes, we returned to Seattle in February 2009. I started my new job back at the World Vision headquarters. Feeling defeated, we pressed on. Because the trip had already been planned, the next month I was in Zambia meeting Esther for the first time.

The summer of 2009 was complicated even further by the fact that Cinnamon was totally burned out from the little eBay business. Liberty Jane had developed a good reputation. Because we focused on branding, built a website and worked hard on our photography, most people thought we were bigger than we really were. I'm not sure it had reached a cult following, but it was close.

But Cinnamon was sewing until midnight trying to keep up with demand. Although the items were popular, we just didn't have a business model that was scalable. With the move to Seattle, and the short sale of our house in California, the financial demands on our little eBay business also went away.

That summer we decided to take a break from eBay; regroup; and ultimately decided to shift the emphasis of Cinnamon's work from making and selling doll clothes, to making and publishing sewing patterns. We began offering her pattern designs as digitally downloaded PDF files. In September 2009 we sold eleven copies of her first pattern.

Liberty Jane Finds Her Way

By 2010 this new strategy really began to work nicely. Instead of trying to take money out of the business, we tried our best to reinvest all the money we could into growing the business. We ended 2010 with total sales of $36,000, triple the prior year.

That year we also had the most fortuitous encounter. Through a mutual friend a Fashion Industry Professor at Seattle Pacific University contacted us. She asked if we could meet. Wow, were we flattered! We had a wonderful meeting. She suggested we meet with one of her friends, Karin, who had been a Senior Designer at Nordstrom for thirteen years. Nordstrom is a legendary Seattle retailer that has a reputation for top designs and incredible customer service.

When we met with Karin, we found a kindred spirit. She was a huge fan of Cinnamon's work, understood the fashion industry at an incredible level, had insane skills, and had left the Nordstrom Product Group the year before. She was so enthusiastic about Cinnamon's work we sensed she might even be interested in working with us. So we took a huge leap of faith, risked embarrassing ourselves, and offered her as much as we could afford. We prayed she'd say yes. Our offer was a fraction of what she would make at a large company, but she could work from home, spend time on fun low-stress projects, and help us build a company.

To our surprise, Karin accepted our offer and became our first employee. Liberty Jane Clothing got a major credibility upgrade. It's not an exaggeration to say that over the next five years, she and Cinnamon went on a design binge that literally transformed the doll clothing industry. I know, you probably didn't know there was a doll clothing industry—and truthfully, maybe there's not. But if there is one, they rocked it. They introduced a level of professionalism and quality of design that set a new standard.

In 2010 we also started to shift the emphasis of Cinnamon's auctions. We slowed way down. When she would make something new, we would auction it and give the funds to Esther. We called these projects *Liberty Jane Gives Back.*

In 2010, I also made a work transition from World Vision to serve as the Senior Vice President of Advancement at Northwest University. I had worked at World Vision for sixteen years—eight years in Human Resources and eight years in fundraising. At Northwest, I was responsible for fundraising, marketing, and Human Resources.

Our First Purposeful Product

That year Esther proposed an exciting project. She proposed that we fund a sewing training program for the moms of the school. They could learn to sew, and maybe in that way increase their income and make items they could sell to support the school.

We agreed to support the program. The funds would be used to purchase some machines, rent a small space, and get a local tailor to train the moms.

During our back-and-forth discussions, they asked if we could help them export the items they were going to make and sell them in

America. I knew that model wouldn't work for a variety of reasons. Instead, we encouraged them to find a local need that they could fill.

We settled on school uniforms for the children. The reason the children didn't have uniforms was because the parents or guardians couldn't afford them. But the tradition in Zambia is that good schools have uniforms. Esther and the moms really wanted Needs Care to be perceived as a quality school. But we couldn't afford to pay for fabric to make uniforms for almost 500 kids.

Then Esther came up with a brilliant suggestion. Instead of giving uniforms to the children as a handout, we could create a small "financing option" where the parents or guardians pay for the uniforms in small payments over time. The cost for each uniform, including a small amount of money for the seamstress's effort, was $14. It allowed the community to participate in the education of their children at an affordable level, in a way that worked for them. It was like Esther's lay-away program for uniforms.

We launched the pilot program, and amazingly, it began to work! The benefits included:

- ✓ The parents or guardians participated financially. To everyone's surprise, this has worked very easily.

- ✓ The school was transformed from a uniform-less to uniformed school. Most community schools don't have uniforms, so the pride and prestige of the Needs Care School skyrocketed. Attendance doubled; as of this writing, attendance is now close to 1,400 students.

- ✓ The students are proud to wear their uniforms and don't have to worry about not having clothing for school.

- ✓ The program gives the seamstresses ongoing income, a product to sell customers, and the pride of knowing they are helping to make the school a better place for their children.

- ✓ We even eventually added a knitting machine (thanks to a generous donation from Shari Fuller at Thimbles &

Acorns), so they can also make custom sweaters for the kids. It's surprisingly cold in Lusaka during their winter (July being the coldest month).

This program took about a year to fully set up, and taught us several important lessons, which we've come to call our "purposeful products" strategy. We've applied these lessons to our Sew Powerful Purse program, which we'll share in upcoming chapters.

But the primary idea behind Purposeful Products is that rather than having seamstresses make tourist trinkets, souvenir shirts, or other non-essential items that are nearly impossible to sell, we try to find ways to have them make items that are essential for the people in Ngombe. In particular, we focus on items that promote educational achievement.

By the end of 2010, we began calling all of this fun activity our "Sew Powerful" project. Cinnamon and I poured our hearts into making doll clothes for auctions, saving enough money for the next phase of the sewing project, and seeing it take small steps forward. It became our passion.

Somehow, working together with Esther and the moms, we had found a way to employ the moms, have them paid for their work by the community, bless the children, and upgrade the prestige of the school.

While most people visit our website and enjoy the pictures of the children at the school, we look at the same pictures and tend to focus on the nice uniforms. It is an incredible contrast from the 2009 pictures. We don't take a single shirt, skirt, or sweater for granted. Each one is a big deal.

In 2011 we tripled our business sales again. We began selling doll clothes patterns for other designers, a few at first, and then a growing number. To our surprise, we had a six figure online business. That felt amazing! We wondered where this little doll clothes business could go. In 2012 we more than doubled sales. In the summer of 2013 we launched Pixie Faire – a marketplace for doll clothes patterns, supplies, and related online classes.

On December 26th, 2013, after waiting more than two years to get it, we also received our IRS Determination Letter granting Sew Powerful

Figure 2.2 *School uniforms - our first purposeful product*

an official Tax-Exempt 501C3 status. Our mission – to combat extreme poverty through sewing education.

When people asked if we were a Faith based organization we would say, "yes – but instead of a focus on evangelism, we are trying to live out James 1:27 – to look after orphans and widows in their time of need."

By 2014 we had more than doubled our annual sales again. I was able to retire from my full-time job and join the growing Liberty Jane/Pixie Faire operation. Our personal goal became to take as little money from the business as possible so we could continue to grow it and grow Sew Powerful.

From 2010 to 2014 we took tiny steps with Sew Powerful, little by little, to organize things, build relationships, strengthen the program, and most importantly ensure that the Zambian seamstresses felt empowered.

In 2014 Sew Powerful received just over $20,000 in charitable giving. We were grateful that people started joining us in supporting the program, but it felt like a tiny amount and not enough to transform Needs Care like we wanted.

The seamstresses in Ngombe were ready for a new challenge since the uniform program was rolling along well. Cinnamon and I began to dream of ways to get more people involved in this important ministry.

Our Unique Structure

You may have heard us call Liberty Jane Clothing the official "big sister" of Sew Powerful. Technically, the set-up we are using is called a Parallel Structure, with the expenses and management of the charity being gifted to Sew Powerful by Liberty Jane Clothing. We didn't want Sew Powerful to be a corporate foundation where the only giving was from Liberty Jane Clothing, or a family foundation either. We wanted it to be a real charitable organization that a lot of donors could support. We didn't know exactly how we were going to get any of those donors involved, but we hoped for the best. If we were going to make a bigger difference, it would take a much larger team.

In simple terms, Liberty Jane Clothing picks up the check on expenses, letting Sew Powerful grow un-burdened by administrative expense. In addition to our personal giving to Sew Powerful, gifted items from Liberty Jane include:

✓ Management and staff

✓ Office space and related expenses and supplies

✓ Marketing expenses

✓ Shipping expenses

Our hope is that one day, Sew Powerful will grow to be much bigger than Liberty Jane Clothing. Someday it will pay its own way in the world; but for now, Liberty Jane is blessed to be able to pay.

We are incredibly honored that from what felt like our personal financial ashes, something creative, fun, and meaningful has blossomed. We're honored to lead a vibrant company and growing charity.

Looking back, we can clearly see how God used our mess to plant the seeds of something that will last much longer than the pain ever did. God has been good to us, and we're going to continue to do our best to transfer those benefits into the lives of the seamstresses and our adopted kids in Ngombe.

PART TWO

Our Stories

"I believe there's a calling for all of us. I know that every human being has value and purpose. The real work of our lives is to become aware. And awakened. To answer the call."

—Oprah Winfrey

October 5th, 1990

By Cinnamon

When people ask me why I focus on the mission and purpose of Sew Powerful, I tell them the story of October 5th, 1990. That's when things changed for me. We each have our own stories related to when God put a burden for others on our heart. Here is my story—a burden for orphans.

On October 5th, 1990, the 20/20 TV Show ran a program on the plight of Romanian orphans raised in state-run orphanages. Do you remember watching it? I was fifteen at the time and trying to figure out what I was going to do with my life.

I remember watching the show having my heart broken for the kids caught in that horrible situation. They were innocent kids. The pictures were gruesome. I was horrified.

It was more than just the sad circumstances I was seeing on the TV that bothered me. For most of my childhood, gymnastics was my passion. My idols were the Romanian athletes that dominated the sport. I tried to copy their moves and dreamed of being as good as them some day. Seeing another side of Romania that night affected me very deeply. What was the difference between the world-class Romanians standing atop the podium at the Olympics and the ones caught in the orphanages? Was it love, care, hugs, and the involvement of caring adults? That hard question has never left me. But I recognized the calling on my life to serve and care for orphans. At that time, I felt so strongly about it that I was convinced I was going to move to Romania and volunteer at an orphanage. The thought of a child neglected and forgotten, never experiencing human touch, became a burden I would always carry.

I spent time during and after high school on various short-term mission trips. Although I didn't feel any of those places or projects was the right thing for me to stick with for the long term, I knew I was gaining valuable experience and insight into different cultures and life circumstances.

After Jason and I got married and started a family, I spent years unsure of how to live out my earlier calling, and how to best integrate it with my new calling to be a wife and mom. My husband and our three amazing children are my priority, but orphans are always on my heart too.

Years later, in 2007, I was finally able to visit Romania. As the plane neared Bucharest for arrival, I had a nervous feeling in my stomach. Could I handle what I was going to encounter?

A lot had changed since 1990. The next week was a whirlwind punctuated by a few intense moments. Several days into the trip we began visiting orphanages and meeting children.

As we stood in an orphanage and got a formal tour, I couldn't help but remember back to that 20/20 special. Although the quality of the buildings and system of care had improved a lot since 1990, many of the kids that grew up in that system were profoundly affected—and still in need of care.

Rodica's Train Ride

We also had the privilege of meeting Rodica and her daughter Andrea, who we'd sponsored for over ten years through World Vision. We had no idea what to expect as we drove out into the countryside. We finally arrived at the small schoolhouse and had a wonderful time together.

Rodica was gracious and upbeat. Her story was hard. She had been abandoned by her husband and was living with her mom who helped her raise her daughter. She did all she could to provide for her.

She had a job, and she left the house each day at 5am to walk two hours to the train station. She rode the train for an hour to get to her job at a factory. After her eight-hour shift, she left work at 5pm and made the return trip. She'd get home after 8pm.

She made $100 USD a month for this effort. But she spent $30 a month on just the train ride. So she netted $70 to survive on.

Now, I know what you might be thinking. Maybe it's easy to live in rural Romania on $70 a month. But you'd be very wrong. The cost of living was surprisingly high. She struggled to survive and provide for her daughter.

As we sat in the schoolhouse, the realization hit me. I had bonded with the World Vision story and mission so deeply because I was trying to "un-break" things that had been broken in my life years before as I watched that 20/20 special. Trying to find and help moms like Rodica. Empowering women with skills to earn a respectable income and provide for their children so that no child was left abandoned, neglected, or un-loved.

Over the years, we watched as Rodica got remarried and had twin daughters. We still sponsor them today. It's one of the highlights of our lives.

Over the next few years I struggled a lot with the frivolous nature of our business. Doll clothes? Really, what in the world was the point of spending my time and energy on that? I knew we needed the income for our family, and we were working to overcome the struggles we were facing; but it didn't really seem like there was a lot of meaning in it.

But as our business began to grow, and I realized we could use the proceeds to "give back," it started to become clear. I didn't need to sell everything, pick up and move to another country to fulfill my calling to serve and care for orphans. I could make a difference with the activities I did each and every day, using the skills and talents God had given me. Not only that, but I could use the platform we had gained by building our brand to tell others the story!

After Jason's trip in 2009, meeting Esther and the kids at Needs Care, we both felt we had adopted 400+ orphans. Now we had our path forward—our small business would be used to help orphans and widows through Sew Powerful. With every design I create, seam I sew, and embellishment I add; God is glorified and lives can be changed. To me that is powerful!

I'm not sure everyone in this world is called by God to serve and care for orphans. But I know we are, and I suspect that if you're reading this book, you are too, and have your own story of how God placed a special burden on your heart to do it. Embrace it. It might be incomplete, but it is not by accident. Write it down and begin believing for amazing next steps. You are uniquely and wonderfully made and the journey that God has taken you on has led you to this moment—a chance to go deep into God's calling in your life. If that means partnering with us through Sew Powerful, then we'll welcome you with open arms.

Lighting Fires
By Jason

I walked into the Human Resources department of World Vision on December 7th, 1994. I was there on a temporary assignment from AppleOne Temporary Agency in Monrovia, California. Cinnamon and I had been married for two months. I stayed at World Vision for sixteen years. It took me several years to really understand why I liked the mission and purpose so much.

Kindred Spirit

I guess you could say I'm a kindred spirit of sorts to orphans. I don't know the pain of loss that they've undergone, but my story has provided me with glimpses.

My dad disappeared when I was nine. He was the Pastor of our local church, and his abandonment of our family shaped my childhood.

It was an odd set of circumstances. Over the course of a few months in 1979, he began to be more withdrawn from us, and would be gone for days at a time.

Then one day, in the summer of 1980, my mom came home and found a long letter that he had written. She found it lying on the bed. His clothes were gone. The note was cryptic and said that he loved us, but that he had to leave. It said that he didn't want to, but that he had to, and that we shouldn't try to find him.

My dad has seven siblings; his mom was still alive at the time too. I remember the night my mom had to go tell them all what happened, show them the letter, and try to explain it. They were nice people, but over the years, we grew apart, as though the link in the chain that was holding us together had broken.

My mom was suddenly on her own with four kids. I was the youngest. She told us she believed he would come back some day. She never lost faith.

She scrambled to pull things together. She even had to go to the church council and resign for him. He made no arrangements related to the church. He just left.

My mom hadn't worked in over ten years. She sold our house and we loaded up the station wagon. In the summer just before I entered fourth grade, we moved to her hometown to be nearer to family.

My siblings all dealt with the trauma in different ways. My mom found peace by going to church three days a week. But going to church was the last thing any of us kids wanted to do.

My coping method was to withdraw and be a cynic. I quickly became an arrogant, over-confident, chip-on-my-shoulder nine-year-old. A certain kind of distrust and rebelliousness got baked into me in the process.

Bruce and Shelley Glines

But a funny thing happened. An amazing couple from the church, Bruce and Shelley Glines, worked hard to win my trust and include me in activities. They were the leaders of the fourth, fifth, and six grade scouting program at the church. I didn't want to go, and my older brothers and sister all refused to go to church. But I was young enough that my mom could still boss me around and make me go. I'm glad she did.

The first night I attended the Wednesday night class, Bruce said he was going to show us how to start a campfire. I had never seen that before, so we followed him out to the little spot he had set up. As we all gathered around the fire pit, he casually pulled a matchbox out of his pocket and struck one match. He said, "it's really pretty easy," and he casually tossed it into the fire pit. The logs erupted in flames. "Wow," everyone screamed. We were all amazed.

Bruce and Shelley started laughing really hard. Then he told us he had soaked the logs in gas before church as a prank—and that we should never actually do that, because it was really dangerous! Then he showed us how to really do it properly. That started my friendship with Bruce and Shelley.

They were like second parents to me, from the time I was in fourth grade until I was twenty-three, when Cinnamon and I got married. Bruce even performed the ceremony.

What made it all possible was a miracle in timing. From fourth through sixth grade, they were my leaders in the scouting program. When I was going into seventh grade, they became the Junior High Pastors at the church, so I continued to go to their programs for the next two years. Then, when I was going into ninth grade, they became the High School Pastors; again I was able to continue along right with them for the next four years.

Throughout Junior High and High School, I found peace in my heart the old-fashioned way—down at the altar of that little church, praying with Bruce and Shelley by my side. Then I'd leave and go hang out with the wrong friends at school, try to walk away from God, and leave religion behind. Then one of them would sit me down and talk with me. I'd ask God to help me find forgiveness and healing. They always had a way of helping me find my way back, never with guilt, judgment, or manipulation. They just cared.

I remember times I would start sobbing almost uncontrollably as they prayed for me. I found healing in those prayers. I found the love of God as my spiritual father. I found a way to trust Him and others. I found peace.

After I graduated from high school, Bruce and Shelley moved a few hours away to become pastors of another church. Bruce asked me if I wanted to join them as an intern. I did, and that transition allowed me to meet Cinnamon, and make the leap into adulthood.

It was the love and support I received from Bruce and Shelley that made a difference in my life. They are people of God, servants and saints.

You're probably still wondering about my dad. Well, seventeen years later, when I was twenty-six, through a bizarre set of circumstances, he came back. He apologized and explained he was living a new life in New York. My parents were divorced and my mom could finally move on. We stay in touch now and occasionally see each other when we can.

A Passion For Caring

I know my passion for helping orphans is somehow tied to deep feelings I harbor in my heart related to my childhood, trying to help kids who are caught in a story they didn't create and don't want. There are a lot of good kids out there that need someone to be there for them.

It's a passion that's also tied to deeply believing in the scriptures that speak about the issue. A few that come to mind include:

> *"Learn to do good; seek justice, correct oppression; bring justice to the fatherless, plead the widow's cause."*
>
> Isaiah 1:17 (ESV)

> *"Religion that God our Father accepts as pure and faultless is this: to look after the orphans and widows in their time of distress."*
>
> James 1: 27 (NIV)

> *"Give justice to the weak and the fatherless; maintain the right of the afflicted and the destitute."*
>
> Psalm 82:3 (ESV)

> *"He pled the cause of the afflicted and needy; then it was well. Is not that what it means to know me? declares the LORD."*
>
> Jeremiah 22:16 (NASB)

> *"For he will deliver the needy who cry out, the afflicted who have no one to help."*
>
> Psalm 72:12 (NIV)

Imagine my surprise when I received this Facebook message not too long ago from my old friend, Shelley Glines: *"Hi Jason, I hope you're well...The ladies from our church want to make 100 purses..."*

Esther's Story

By Esther Mkandawire

My names are *Esther Chizya Mkandawire*, I am the seventh born in a family of eleven, and we are seven women and four men. My father used to work for the mines. He grew up as an orphan from the age of six, and he died in 2001.

Due to his upbringing, he trained us to love and care for anyone in life, whether a friend or stranger, poor or rich. He always said we should treat everyone the same, as we are all one in God's image.

I did my primary school at the Nampundwe mine, where my father was working at the time. Upon reaching grade seven, I was to go to a secondary school or high school in another location, as where we were staying there was none. But due to my age, the schools refused me because I was young and so small.

This was the turning point of my life. I grew up as a loved child where everything was available for me. Life was easy and good for me. My father valued education so much that he never allowed us to do any household chores; all we needed to do was study. So my attendance at secondary school was like fulfilling his dream, as I was his first girl child to reach this far. My elder siblings had refused to go to school and were married at a young age. Everyone in the family was happy, and they all encouraged me to really study hard. I wanted to be a nurse to help people in the hospitals.

My uncle was staying in Lusaka and he proposed that I come and stay with him and attend secondary school. He was doing very fine in life; he even had his own company. So I moved to Lusaka. Things changed a lot when I moved into their home. I had to start cleaning plants, sweeping the house and the yard, and washing my cousins' clothes. Life became so hard for me. I used to cry day and night, but it was all in vain.

I wanted to leave my uncle's place and go back to my family, but it was too far; I didn't have the money, and I didn't know how to arrange it. Looking back, I strongly thank my father because he made me get educated and get strong. He used to trick me into staying. Every time he came through, and I complained about how I was being treated, he would assure me that he was going to take me back to the village. But then he'd casually leave and say, "I just going to go get you a new bag so you can pack up your things." A year later he'd come back and play the same trick on me.

Eventually I became used to the life of a housemaid. Every time the maid stopped work or the garden boy left his job, I would be put in charge of their work. My cousins were older than me, so they would make me do everything for them. I was given a lot of chores with no time to rest, or read. This became part of my life and I had no one to complain to.

After graduating from secondary school, I really wanted to be a nurse, but again I was refused this opportunity. So I was advised to do dressmaking and designing, which I obtained a diploma in.

Because of the life situation at my uncle's house, I got married at the age of 19 and had my first born at 20.

Life was okay for us. My husband was working for a military firm, and we were able to meet most of our basic needs. I ended up having five children. I have two girls who are now grown women, and three boys. The girls have their diploma in Social Work and Counseling. My first-born is now doing her last year in Library Science studies at the University. My second-born daughter is working with me, since she has a degree in social work and counseling. My eldest son wants to do agriculture or mechanics. The fourth wants to do medicine as a doctor, and my baby boy is at Needs Care School in seventh grade.

I became involved in this work by the grace of God. The reason I say that is because I never did project management in my life. I have never been a teacher before, or school administrator. But I started this school from nothing; all I can say is that it is a calling from God.

I started it in 2003 after noticing that there were a lot of children here in Ng'ombe who were not going to school. We had moved here with the intention of buying our own land and building a house of our own, because we had been renters before that. After I noticed all the children who weren't attending school, I approached a friend about it. She explained more about the type of life that was going on in this community, the lack of government schools, and the overall situation.

So I told my friend that since I was not doing anything else, I was just a full-time house wife, why not start up something for these vulnerable children? We started approaching churches to see if we could use one for the location of the school. Fortunately, the Reformed Church in Zambia gave us a space. So in August 2003 we started with 96 children. Currently we have over 1450 children coming to learn every day at Needs Care Community School. What inspires me most in this work is to put a smile on the orphans' and vulnerable children's faces. We also provide a daily meal for the children.

We also use the school for adult literacy classes and a sewing cooperative program. The ladies make the school uniforms and hygiene supplies so the girls can stay in school all month.

We also have a clinic and a group of 90 caregivers who do outreach programs visiting the homes of the children at our school and helping those who are chronically ill. Though we can't provide for all their needs, we can at least put a smile on their faces by encouraging them with life and sharing God's word. We have so many that are HIV positive. This is what really keeps me going. I have such a passion for the needy.

We have eight teachers, two cooks and eleven seamstresses. We have a security guard, several medical personnel for our clinic and a farm caretaker.

My traditional name is Chizya Cha Landa. *Chizya* means *slave, cha* means *for, landa* means *needy.* And it's true, I have a passion for serving the vulnerable groups.

I could write a book if I had time to share my experiences in this wonderful work! Thank you so much for coming to our aid; we are so humbled by your support.

PART THREE

The Sew Powerful Purse

"*Philanthropy is not about the money. It's about using whatever you have at your fingertips and applying them to improve the world.*"

—Melinda Gates

Our Second Purposeful Product

By Jason

In early 2014 an opportunity to return to Zambia presented itself, and we were excited to go. It was time for Cinnamon to finally meet Esther, see Ngombe, and spend time with the seamstresses.

I hadn't seen Esther since 2009 or even seen the new school building or sewing room. Cinnamon and I were excited to go together. She hadn't ever been to Africa, so this was going to be a fun adventure.

Amazing Progress

Esther and the group of moms had accomplished so much since 2009. The partially completed church was a distant memory, although it is just across the street from the new school, so they still use it for large program events.

By 2014 Program milestones included:

✓ A nice new school was completed.

✓ 1,200 children were happily attending.

✓ All the children were wearing their nice blue uniforms.

✓ The moms had turned into seamstresses and were paid for their work, which benefited them personally as well as the school.

✓ The school has cooks that prepare a simple meal of porridge for the children each day.

✓ They had begun receiving funds from a Seattle-area doctor for a part-time nurse, so a small clinic was opened in a house across from the school.

✓ An adult literacy program was conducted in the afternoons.

✓ The seamstresses had even begun their own charitable project, giving their practice clothing items to a very rural village where the children didn't have much clothing.

Headed to Zambia

The reason we were able to go to Zambia was because Northwest University had a summer missions trip program. As I looked at the locations they were offering, I noticed there wasn't any program in Southern Africa. So I offered to lead a team as long as Cinnamon could go too. The Chaplain said that if I could get at least five students to go, the university would cover my trip costs as the team leader, and they could make it an official trip. I wrote up a simple description:

> *"Ngombe Compound in Lusaka is an incredibly intense urban slum in the country of Zambia. It has a massively high HIV/AIDS rate; most the children are orphans, and yet, amazing things are happening there at a place called the Needs Care School. If you want to join us, meet the kids, learn about the medical, social, and economic issues, then sign up for this trip."*

We had five nursing students sign up, and one teaching student. Our trip was confirmed. We were thrilled! While the nursing students participated in clinic duties, and the teaching student participated in teaching duties, Cinnamon would spend time working with the seamstresses. My job was to serve as the team leader, take pictures, and coordinate all the various details.

Back at Needs Care

On May 28th, 2014, we finally got to see the new school, sewing room, spend time getting to know the seamstresses and see their work firsthand. We were excited that the uniform program was working well, the team was strong, and the seamstresses were ready for another challenge.

The sewing team had started to grow and included a head seamstress and a head knitter. We had done several six-month training sessions at that point, with a paid outside instructor, and a total of forty ladies had gone through the sewing training program.

Returning to Ngombe that first day felt incredible. Cinnamon was finally able to see the place we had spent five years supporting. To my surprise, the welcome ceremony was conducted in the church the school had used for so many years. Seeing it complete was a nice surprise. The children sang for us and welcomed us with a huge celebration.

That night our schedule worked out so that we could have dinner with an old friend. Chikondi Phiri was a Zambian that I had attended graduate school with from 2000 to 2004. He hadn't been in Lusaka when we visited in 2009, but it was fun to see him again. He and his wife came and shared with our group over dinner.

The graduate degree program we attended was part of a leadership effort that World Vision had coordinated. Each summer our cohort would meet in Toronto, Canada, as an intensive MBA program with an emphasis in non-profit management. Chikondi and I were roommates the first year by random chance, and then again by random chance the second year. Our friendship was set. I learned an amazing amount from Chikondi in those four years.

When we reconnected that night in Lusaka almost ten years later, we didn't skip a beat. Chikondi was a senior leader in the World Vision Zambia office now. His wife Anne joined us, and she and Cinnamon immediately hit it off. We enjoyed a great dinner, and their insights into Ngombe were incredibly helpful as well. They wanted to know all about what we were doing and offered their support.

Lunch Lessons

On the second day, Esther asked us to help serve the children lunch. It was a simple scoop of porridge. The World Food Program was providing the food, but the moms would buy firewood to cook it, and brown sugar to add to it. We watched as the children brought their small plastic containers and lined up. They each got a scoop and went and sat in groups on the ground. Esther said,

> *"If you notice, they only eat part of it, and then put the lid on their container and take the rest home. They share it with their family. These families have literally no food in their houses. It is our biggest issue."*

We were in shock. First, it was a very humble scoop of porridge. I like cream of wheat, but these kids needed more than that. Esther went on to explain,

> *"With so many children, we have a hard time getting enough food, cooking it all, and even then, it's not nutritious enough. Most of these children are Positive [meaning HIV Positive], so they need good nutrition or their Anti-Retroviral drugs won't work. The drugs upset their stomachs if they take them on an empty stomach; so without getting them more food, we are cutting their chances of survival. It makes us so sad."*

We left that conversation depressed. There was simply no way we could fund this project. With 1,200 children, even a humble budget of .50 cents per child, per day, would cost $3,000 a week.

Our Work Begins

The students began participating in their projects, and Cinnamon began spending time with the seamstresses. She had planned to teach them how to make simple girl's dresses, but then she walked into their storage room.

What she discovered was box after box of XXXL sized men's pants and shirts. World Vision Zambia had donated it to the ladies because they couldn't find a use for it. They thought maybe the ladies would want to use it as fabric scraps or could somehow find a use for the material. But the seamstresses didn't know what to do with it, didn't want to ruin it, so it had sat unused.

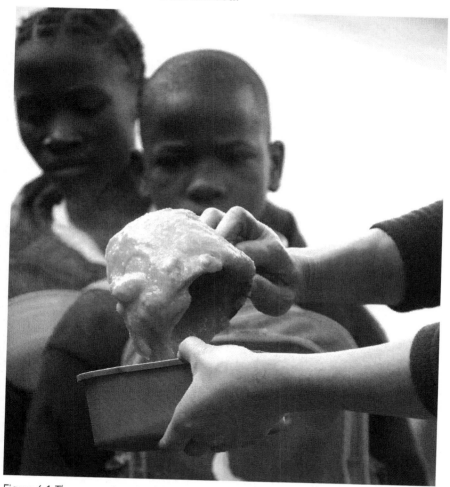

Figure 6.1 *The expressions on the faces say it all*

I was already very familiar with the process of American manufacturers donating unsold clothing to World Vision. The clothing would be accepted as a donation, referred to as Gifts-In-Kind, and used at program locations around the world. What we didn't know until that day was that World Vision would receive, and not have a use for, the extremely large sizes. Very few people in developing countries like Zambia have a need for clothing made for very large men.

As you might guess, Cinnamon knew exactly what to do with this goldmine of fabric. That afternoon she put on a workshop for cutting down the garments and making a collection of child-sized items. The energy in the room was ecstatic as she gave the ladies the confidence and techniques to chop things up and repurpose them.

Figure 6.2 *Those are pretty big pants*

She quickly showed them how to keep the shirt collars intact, size and cut down the body of the shirts, and transform them into boy-sized shirts. The extra fabric turned into girl-sized skirts.

Cinnamon noticed that one of the ladies had a nice messenger bag and another had a nice book bag. She showed them how to use them as patterns, and turn the enormous man-sized pants into messenger bags and book bags. The next morning, we returned to begin another fun day with the seamstresses. To our surprise, we saw stacks and stacks of the items. They had worked hard all evening, had taken Cinnamon's ideas, and expanded on them to make even more creative pieces. We realized they were extremely talented and not shy about making items once they got the idea.

Figure 6.3 *Seamstresses learning new skills*

The ladies still make these items occasionally, but it was fairly easy for our friends at World Vision to integrate those concepts into their own sewing program; the Needs Care seamstresses rarely get those items anymore. We certainly don't fault them for that—we were honored to help find a purpose for those items.

Reusable Feminine Hygiene Pads

That summer we realized we needed a second purposeful product that the seamstresses could make in larger quantities. It needed to have the same purposeful product attribute that we had discovered with the school uniforms. It needed to be an essential item and meet a need at the school, or at least in Ngombe. It needed to be easy for the seamstresses to make and be in fairly high demand.

We also needed to find a way beyond our charity auctions for a larger number of donors to start getting involved in Sew Powerful. As our business grew over the years we found that there was a meaningful percentage of our customers that liked this topic, wanted to know what we were doing, and wanted to be involved; but we didn't have any practical way for them to participate on a regular basis.

After we returned home, we met for the first time with a new group we had decided to set up as our Board of Directors. It included:

✓ Dana Buck, a Senior Director at World Vision

✓ Andy Smith, an Executive Pastor from Walnut Creek

✓ Toby Capps, a sales representative for McKesson

✓ Kevin LaRoche, a pastor on staff at our church

These were all long-time friends. In fact, Dana, Andy, and Toby had been with me on the original trip to Ngombe in 2009.

We described the trip, the amazing progress at both the school and sewing cooperative, and explained our hopes related to next steps for the program. One of our board members mentioned that he had seen a charity that made reusable feminine hygiene products, and he wondered if that might be a good match for the seamstresses. Then we asked the question, *"How can we include seamstresses from around the world in this project?"*

Cinnamon had the winning idea. Years before she had made a very cute cross body purse and had the pattern pieces. She said we could publish it for free, ask our customers to download it, make one, and send it to us. If we could figure out how to send them to Zambia, then we could have the seamstresses there make the feminine hygiene product, and give it to the girls with a cute purse.

We had no idea whether this was a valid idea or not, whether the girls in Ngombe needed the product, whether the seamstresses would want to make it, how we would send the purses, and how much any of it would cost. But it was an exciting idea we decided to begin looking into.

The next day we saw a shocking statistic published by the Duke University Global Health Initiative:

In Kenya, girls reported they can miss between 3–7 days of school each month because of their period. They have no product, so they simply stay home.

We wondered if that same statistic would be true for the girls at Needs Care. We asked Esther, and told her about the program idea. Her response was, *"Yes, we have this same situation here. The girls have no product to use so they stay home."*

Next we asked Esther if there was any way to validate the impact of this situation through test results and she said, *"Yes, we have the 7th Grade exam scores and they show that girls don't perform as well as boys."*

As background (for Americans) in sub-Saharan Africa, the school system includes two stages: "primary school" and "secondary school." Primary school includes grades 1–7, what we call "elementary school." It is completed with a major state test that determines whether or not you are eligible to attend secondary school, which is what we in America call "high school." It includes grade 8–12.

If you pass the 7th grade exam, you have the academic right to attend secondary school. (Of course, you still have to be able to do it financially and socially.) But if you fail it, you are done with your formal schooling. Esther's data showed that on average, over the last several years, her girls fail that test at 10% higher rates than boys. We were shocked.

What's The Impact?

We discovered there is a large body of research related to secondary school attendance and major life outcomes. Social scientists have documented significant impact of not attending secondary school. We were shocked to learn that, according to the U.N.:

- ✓ If all girls attended secondary school, pregnancies under the age of 17 would drop by 60%.
- ✓ Teen girls who drop out before completing secondary school are four times more likely to contract HIV.
- ✓ Educated women have on average 3.9 children compared to 5.3 children for those who drop out before completing secondary school.
- ✓ Teen girls that attend secondary school have 70% fewer teenage marriages than those who drop out.

We also began asking advice and counsel from wise community development practitioners, and health care industry professionals. We even met with people interested in the issue of MHM (Menstruation Hygiene Management) at various charities. We didn't even know that term existed until we started to research it more.

Product Options

There are two commonly used personal care items for women in Zambia, as well as most African nations. There are disposable products or reusable products.

The reusable product comes in two versions. There is a "traditional" version that has been used for many years, and is used by the women of Zambia. We won't go into detail, but interestingly we've heard from older American women that it is the same method they used prior to the invention of disposable products.

But there are also newly designed versions of reusable pads and liners that are elegant, leak resistant if not leak proof, and easily washable.

Why Not Disposables?

One option, which none of the poor use, is a disposable product just like women use in the western world. These products are readily available on every grocery store shelf throughout Zambia. There is no shortage of supply. So, depending on their proximity to a grocery store, they do have this option. Of course many rural villages don't have a grocery store anywhere nearby. The major problem is the cost. This is a very expensive solution and poorer women cannot afford it.

Then there is the ecological problem involved in using disposable products in a place like Ngombe. Even if they could afford to use disposable products, with no garbage service in their community, these products would create an ecological nightmare as they are thrown into the out-house, or placed into the open sewage areas. Thankfully disposable baby diapers aren't used in Ngombe either.

Interestingly, this same problem impacts the urban poor, but it also impacts the rural poor. In a very rural setting the women and teen girls would not have the ability to get disposable product; even if they did, its use would create an ecological problem. In that context the trash would be burned, but it still isn't a good environmental practice.

Sadly, in our research and interviews, we discovered there are African companies and charities that are trying to advocate and dispense disposable products in both urban and rural settings. We believe they are betting on the wrong solution.

Our questions for the charity leaders promoting this solution are:

✓ What is a girl supposed to do when your charity goes out of existence, she moves, or for other reasons, she cannot come get your free gift?

✓ What is the ecological impact of your solution and how can that be justified?

Our conclusion is that disposables are a western convenience product that doesn't translate into poor communities. Simply "gifting" disposable pads into poor communities won't solve a very complex situation.

Why Reusables?

We found two organizations that had pioneered work using a reusable product approach. Both have models that we could learn from. So we reached out to both, had meetings and discussions, and began studying their approach.

The Days for Girls Approach: One is a charity in Washington not too far from us, called Days For Girls. We have a ton of respect for them and what they've accomplished. They publish pattern pieces and ask women from around the world to sew reusable pads and a simple drawstring bag, and then distribute them through local partners such as schools and missions' teams.

The Afripads Approach: The other organization is a for-profit company in Uganda called Afripads. They started much like we did, trying to make a sewing opportunity available to a group of women. Their strategy was to hire local sales representatives and begin selling the reusable product through retailers as well as to non-profit organizations.

Our Approach: What we settled on was an elegantly designed and constructed reusable pad and liner as the best solution. They are easily washed and reused, and just the type of item our seamstresses could make quickly and easily.

There are two pieces involved—a shield and a liner. The liner is inserted into the shield, placed in the underwear and closed with a snap. The shield is constructed with a layer of waterproof material.

We had been to the fabric district in Lusaka, so we knew that there was material available that could be used to make these items. We estimated that each girl would need two shields and eight liners. But we still had a lot of unanswered questions.

With Esther's encouragement, and assurance that the seamstresses would love the new product if we could come and teach them how to make it, we moved forward and finished the Sew Powerful Purse pattern. Would any of our customers be willing to make purses and send them to us? Could we link seamstresses from around the world to join us in this effort? We literally had no idea, but our hopes were high.

The Sew Powerful Purse

By Jason

*W*e launched our Sew Powerful Purse pattern on July 17th, 2014, in our weekly Liberty Jane Newsletter, and asked that purses be sent to us by October 1st. We really had no idea if anyone would be interested, but we announced a goal of 1,011 purses by October 11th, which was International Girls Day.

We are fortunate that we have an enthusiastic customer base of seamstresses that supports our work at Liberty Jane and Pixie Faire, our pattern marketplace. At the time our email list was about 50,000 seamstresses, and they were used to us including small updates about Sew Powerful. But we had never asked for anything like this before.

We explained the program, asked them to do us a favor, and consider making a purse for a worthy cause. But we were really nervous that no one would take the time to make such a complicated purse as a gift for a girl on the other side of the world. Each purse takes a couple hours to make.

To make sure we got people's attention, we set up and personally funded a trip contest. If you made a purse you'd be entered into a drawing and could win a trip to Zambia with us in May 2015. We thought if nothing else, it would definitely get people talking.

We also asked that each purse maker take the time to include a personal note to the girl that would receive the purse. We asked them to take their time and focus on quality. We hoped they would realize how desperate these girls were and how big a gift this would be. We wanted them to make sure the purse and note were truly heartfelt.

On the first day, over 1,200 people downloaded the free purse pattern. That felt like a good start. As the date got closer, the boxes started to pour in. We had them go to our P.O. box, and then I picked them up. We began to receive encouraging comments via email and social media. With each one we felt more and more like we had found a way to include our customers in the mission of Sew Powerful.

During August and September I'd go to the post office each week and collect the packages. The Post Office ladies started to get mad at me for the volume of packages they had to deal with. Sometimes there would be a dozen at a time, which felt like a lot.

I tried to explain to them that it was for charity, but they didn't seem to care. I don't really blame them; there is always a really long line at our post office and I was always too embarrassed to explain the feminine hygiene part of the project to them. Each week I kept wondering whether understanding the full program would make a difference for them. Mostly though, I was just thrilled there were packages each week. It felt like I was Santa's helper for the girls of Ngombe.

Our First Unboxing Party

On the night of October 1st, we gathered at the house of one of our board members, Toby Capps, and asked a few friends from church to help us open all the packages and boxes. Toby and his wife Janairie had been with me on the trip to Ngombe in 2009, so our program was near and dear to their hearts. It took us several hours to open all the boxes, write notes if one wasn't included, remove the occasional piece of candy, and put the purses in the shipping boxes so they could be sent to Zambia.

We took our time and marveled over the creativity of what we saw. We really had no idea what to expect. It seemed like each package was filled with beautiful, intricate, high-quality purses. They were shockingly good.

Figure 7.1 *The first un-boxing party*

At the end of the night we had counted 388 purses, well short of our goal of 1,000. But we were anything but disappointed. We were blown away by the love and care that had gone into each purse. They were amazing, and even the note cards were heartfelt and sincere.

Toward the end of the night, as we were unboxing the purses, someone asked me why I had made the goal 1,000. I said, *"October 11th was International Girls Day, so I thought 1,011 would be a great number."*

Then they asked, *"How many girls at the Needs Care School will need a purse?"*

I had to admit that I wasn't sure. Our program wasn't an exact science at that point. I said, *"Well, they have 1,200 students from grades 1–7, so I'd imagine they have several hundred girls in grade 5, 6, and 7. So, maybe we have enough purses. Maybe we even have some extra."*

"What are you going to do with the extra purses if there are more than the girls at Needs Care can use?"

"Um, I'm not sure..."

No one seemed to mind too much that I didn't have exact answers. I think they all realized we were making this up as we went along. Each question planted a seed in my mind that would grow into a future challenge to overcome. But the challenges seemed incredibly exciting.

Over the next few weeks we received more purses, and we ended up collecting 503 in total during 2014. We received request after request from seamstresses around the world asking us if this was a one-time project, or if we were going to continue it into 2015 and beyond. Although there was no question in our mind, we still hadn't actually distributed the purses in Zambia, worked with the seamstresses there to make the reusable pads, or seen the health training. So we were stepping out in faith and had a lot of work ahead of us.

But Is Our Purse a Good Development Idea?

For several months we began to deeply consider the overall approach we were beginning to implement. I believe each of us struggles with knowing how to show care for others in an effective way. We all have our opinions about the best way to do things, from Bill and Melinda Gates with their billion-dollar annual charity budget, to the fixed-income grandma.

We all have family members that need our help and support. Sometimes our community needs our help and support. Then of course, there are also the orphans in far-off places. How do we respond to the issues we see in places like Africa?

Sadly, there are tons of people who are self-focused to an extreme, spending all their time and energy trying to find happiness in another trip to the mall, another expensive purse, car, or fancy meal. Even mission trips can be a form of self-indulgence.

Who To Help and How To Help Them

Usually though, at some point, we achieve a bit of success in life, we grow up a little, and even the most selfish people move into the make-meaningful-contributions phase of life. It is at that point we face the dilemma of who to help and how to help them.

This isn't a new issue, of course. When a scholar stood up to test Jesus about his views on eternal life, Jesus' first response was to confirm that he understood the Jewish belief system for going to Heaven, *"Love the Lord your God with all your heart, and love your neighbor as yourself."*

The expert in the law pushed back, by asking the question, *"Who is my neighbor?"* In other words, *"Who am I supposed to love as much as I love myself?"*

Jesus responded with this well-known story we call the Good Samaritan. As you read it again, consider these questions,

Question #1 - Who am I supposed to demonstrate love toward?

Question #2 - How am I supposed to be of help?

> *"A man was going down from Jerusalem to Jericho, when he was attacked by robbers. They stripped him of his clothes, beat him and went away, leaving him half dead.*
>
> *A priest happened to be going down the same road, and when he saw the man, he passed by on the other side.*
>
> *So too, a Levite, when he came to the place and saw him, passed by on the other side.*
>
> *But a Samaritan, as he traveled, came where the man was; and when he saw him, he took pity on him. He went to him and bandaged his wounds, pouring on oil and wine. Then he put the man on his own donkey, brought him to an inn and took care of him.*
>
> *The next day he took out two denarii and gave them to the innkeeper. 'Look after him,' he said, 'and when I return, I will reimburse you for any extra expense you may have.'*
>
> *Which of these three do you think was a neighbor to the man who fell into the hands of robbers?*
>
> *The expert in the law replied, 'The one who had mercy on him.'*
>
> *Jesus told him, 'Go and do likewise.' "*

Here are my reflections. I've broken them down to focus on the two primary questions of "who" and "how."

Answering The Who Question

It's Not Just Family Bound: Jesus constructed this story to ensure we saw helping others as something that is not tied to just our family relationships. Of course, I'm not saying we shouldn't care for our immediate family members; of course we should. But this story suggests we shouldn't stop there. We should have the mental and emotional maturity to envision a future where we are helping people outside our immediate family.

It's Not Just Community Bound: Jesus goes out of his way to describe the people in his story by region in order to prove a very specific point. You should be helpful to people regardless of whether they are from your tribe or not. We should get over our prejudices, stereotypes, and biases and not let them hold us back from doing what is right.

We occasionally get a response back to Sew Powerful emails that goes something like this:

> *"There is a lot of need here in the U.S. Why don't you focus your purse project in America?"*

Our response is always the same:

> *"We feel a burden for Zambia, so that is where we focus; but we'd love to have you use our purse pattern and program model to make a difference in your community—let us know how it goes!"*

It's About Who God Puts In Your Path: It might sound simplistic, but my interpretation of the Good Samaritan story is that we are supposed to help the people in need that God puts in our life path. When we encounter them, we are supposed to respond in a very specific way, which we should call using our resources to provide extravagant love and care.

It's About Who Catches Your Eye and Breaks Your Heart: I don't believe we are called to care for every single circumstance we encounter in life. If we did, we would be overwhelmed, spread way too thin, and ultimately ineffective.

Jesus said the Good Samaritan *"came where the man was; and when he saw him, he took pity on him."*

Is it wrong to think that God has a few specific charitable assignments in your life that he wants you to invest into in a deep way, and that when you see them your heart will know it?

Could it be that he'll orchestrate the events of your life, your skills, talents and your creative energy to be a perfect match for helping achieve a specific charitable mission? I think so.

But How Are We Supposed to Help?

Demonstrating Love and Care: The Good Samaritan story outlines a series of actions that the Good Samaritan took in response to the situation. It was not simply handing the guy a $5 bill and saying, "God Bless."

The story shows a series of wise actions and responses that demonstrated genuine love and care. This wasn't simply about absolving himself of the duty of responding; this guy actually demonstrated awesome, beautiful, deeply authentic care in a way that was effective. How did he do it?

Participation: Jesus said, *"He went to him."* I've found that one of the hardest things to do is to be in the presence of trauma. There are two types of emergencies. The first is a rapid-onset emergency, like a hurricane. The second is a slow-onset emergency like HIV/AIDS. But demonstrating true care means being willing to go into the emergency and get involved via thoughtful and wise action. That's a commitment of time as well as mental and emotional energy. Money isn't necessarily the primary response tool.

Using What You Have to Show You Care: Did you ever wonder where the Good Samaritan got the bandages? I'd imagine he made them on the fly out of some nice materials that he had with him. Imagine that, even the Good Samaritan had a stash of fabric!

Jesus said, *"He bandaged his wounds, pouring oil and wine."* Obviously that means the Good Samaritans had items that he was willing to give to the needy person.

He gave items that were used to directly solve an obvious need and he was willing to give it as part of his authentic care. We should meditate on this idea. I believe,

> When we make supporting the needy a money-only proposition, we eliminate the creativity, talent, and application of life experiences that God has given us.

First Responders: Jesus said, *"Then he put the man on his own donkey, brought him to an inn and took care of him."* It's common that people in trauma are unable to administer good solutions. It's a function of their stress and being overwhelmed. The Good Samaritan dealt with the immediate trauma effectively.

Organizers of Longer-Term Plans: Jesus said, "The next day he took out two denarii and gave them to the innkeeper. *'Look after him,'* he said, *'and when I return, I will reimburse you for any extra expense you may have.'"*

Finding and implementing long-term solutions isn't about having money, it is about having a plan. It is about expressing love and care in a dedicated way: *"A long obedience in the same direction,"* to borrow a phrase from Eugene Peterson.

Of course, we like to say, *"The Good Samaritan must have been rich to do all of this stuff."* But the story doesn't indicate that he was a rich person. It just indicates that he was willing to give in a meaningful and thoughtful way.

Mistakes to Avoid

Some skeptics have wisely asked, *"Can't our giving actually hurt the recipient?"* Truth is, many donors have come to realize that giving can go very wrong. There are several negative issues that can arise in the process. As it turns out, giving can damage the giver, and it can also damage the receiver. How? Consider these mistakes to avoid,

A Messiah Complex in The Heart of the Giver: There is a huge opportunity for the giver to begin to feel superior and assume that he is special. People call this a "Messiah Complex," even though my Messiah was a humble and gracious servant. Unfortunately, when ego gets involved, things can get ugly. There is nothing worse than a rich egomaniac going on a crusade to help the poor. No one wants to work with a self-absorbed giver.

Dependency on the Part of the Receiver: Any parent raising a teenager can tell you there is a balancing act that must be managed. It's a balance between meeting needs in kindness and enabling bad behavior. Struggle makes people stronger.

We want to help meet the needs of people; but on the other hand, we want to ensure they are honest, self-reliant, prepared for life's challenges, strong, and successful in life.

Robbing Parents and Community of the Dignity of Self Improvement

We are not the parents of the poor children of Ngombe. Even if we adopt them in our heart, we still need to honor the role of the guardians and local community in their care. If long-term friendship and collaboration are going to develop, there has to be an equal partnership based on trust and mutual respect.

Falling for Guilt Trips by Abusers: Abusers manipulate others by preying on their generosity, and in that way they aren't good partners. They don't demonstrate respect in the process; and in our view, it disqualifies them from ongoing support.

The victim on the Jericho road was a real victim of actual trauma. Abusers manipulate these ideas to try to force you into supporting their poor lifestyle choices. They get a "free pass" on being judged, or working to turn their life around; and you get the permanent assignment to comply with their wishes in support of their particular vice. That's wrong.

We all need to be liberated from guilt trips and have the emotional, spiritual and social power to speak the truth in love. We need to get smart about our charitable efforts.

Power Imbalance: There is a funny version of the Golden Rule that people sometimes use to explain a relational power imbalance. It is, *"He who has the gold makes the rules."* That's a funny way of describing what can be a serious problem.

Donors can frequently get a sense of superiority and begin imposing all sorts of burdens on the recipient. It must be guarded against.

Destroying Markets: Large-scale programmatic giving can easily destroy local markets. We want to avoid this in both the school uniform market and the reusable feminine hygiene product market. We'd rather see local industry in Zambia thrive, and figure out how to be a part of that industry, than grow a large western charity.

It's true that we donate our reusable feminine hygiene products to schoolgirls. But the seamstresses making the product are paid a good wage to make it—and in that way, we are developing a market, rather than destroying it. Donations to our program make that possible and in the future we believe these items will also be sold locally adding another income source.

We are in the business of employing seamstresses to make purposeful products. We want customers to pay for our products. In this way we foster local economies, rather than hurting them.

Our Program Oath

Robert Lupton of FCS Urban Ministries created an insightful oath, which we've modified and adapted for our own use. As we work with the sewing cooperative participants, and other program recipients, we will focus on these principles:

> *We won't do for others what they have the capacity to do for themselves.*

> *We co-create programs with community members. We are not bosses, and they are not our workers. We are partners.*

> *We will respect the skills, experiences, and abilities our partners have in solving problems in their community, and not assume we know what is best.*

The Sew Powerful Purse

We will work to make the seamstresses, teachers, and moms the heroes of the story and empower them to support their sons and daughters with dignity and skill.

We will work to listen and carefully assess both spoken and unspoken needs of our partners, so our actions will ultimately strengthen rather than weaken the hand of those we serve.

Above all, we will work to the best of our ability to do no harm.

The Sew Powerful Promise

By Jason

*O*ur first challenge after receiving the 503 purses was how to get them to Zambia. Thankfully I had a board member that worked at World Vision, and we had good relationships there. Since it was just a few boxes, they offered to ship the purses for free via their container system. That was an incredible help.

Our First Purse Distribution

May 2015 came quickly and we were excited to return to Zambia. The 503 purses had arrived a few weeks before we did and the stage was set for the launch of our program. We had purses, seamstresses, and we had girls that needed to stay in school all month. Now it was time to put it all together.

The 2015 trip included my mom and stepdad, Cinnamon, myself, Melinda, one of our employees at Liberty Jane, and Karen Loke. Karen was the winner of our make-a-purse contest. Cinnamon was excited to have Melinda and Karen on the trip so they could help teach the seamstresses the process of making the reusable shields and liners.

We arrived at the school on the first day and were warmly greeted. The children sang for us, the seamstresses sang for us, and this year they even put on a play. It was a skit designed for the girls of the school, to make sure they knew to report abuse.

By 2015 I realized that Esther was using our annual arrival as an opportunity to have the children prepare and perform songs, poems, and now skits that they worked on for several months. We were there to cheer them on.

Scooping The Porridge

Lunch came quickly, and as with the prior year, we helped serve the children their meal. This time Esther shared bad news. She explained that the lunches weren't able to happen each day because food from the World Food Program was not being donated regularly. So on those days, the children got nothing for lunch, and frequently ate nothing that day. It seems the school lunch program had gone from bad to worse.

Shouts of Joy

That afternoon Cinnamon, Karen, and Melinda began explaining the project and showing the seamstresses the new product pieces using material we had brought with us. By the end of the first afternoon, all the seamstresses were cutting fabric, making shields and liners, and starting to figure out the construction steps. It was so exciting to see the program start to come together.

The plan was that the seamstresses would sew enough shields and liners that week for the teachers to conduct a health class on Thursday, so we could actually go through the entire process of distributing purses to girls.

But we could tell there was still a little bit of confusion in the minds of the seamstresses by the questions they were asking. Esther had assured us that this product was urgently needed, that the seamstresses would be completely supportive, but something seemed off. After a few more questions, Cinnamon realized they didn't understand what they were making. They had never seen this type of product before and the shapes of the pieces didn't make sense to them.

Cinnamon wisely took the shields and liners, showed them exactly how they worked together, and the seamstresses burst out into laughter, clapping, and dancing. Up until that moment, they didn't understand how the product would be used.

Suddenly the room was filled with energy. Several of them said, *"We need this product too."* Their desire to figure out the sewing work was raised to a more intense, exciting level. They had just discovered how to solve a real problem with their sewing machines, and they were incredibly motivated. There was no stopping them!

That night as a team we discussed it all and quickly came to the realization that the seamstresses should each get a purse too. In fact, it only seemed right that they should be the first to benefit from the program.

We returned the next day, and as you might guess, there were stacks of pads and holders that had been sewn. The seamstresses had worked all evening to make as many as possible. We knew that with their enthusiasm this was going to be a hit product.

That morning we went to the local garment district and began sourcing local materials and pricing everything out. We found everything we needed to complete the shields and liners, and it was all commonly available in large quantities right in Lusaka.

Overcoming Obstacles

Esther was thrilled with how it was all coming together, but on the second day as we sat in the sewing room she said, *"I have a few concerns. Most girls here only have one or two pair of underwear, so we need to include several pair of underwear in the purses if possible."*

The thought had never occurred to us, but of course it made sense.

She went on to say, *"There is no soap in these people's houses to wash these items, so we are going to need to include soap as well."*

That made sense too. Then she said, *"I have another concern that is harder to resolve. The moms, aunties, or older sisters of these girls are never going to let them keep these items. They are too valuable. They will take them from the girls and use them for themselves."*

That day at lunch our group talked about this last issue. In a way it made us sad. We hadn't realized how valuable these purses and reusable pads would be. But in a way, it also validated the worth and importance of the product idea. As a group we came up with a solution and suggested it to Esther.

We said, *"What if each girl receives two purses; one purse for their own use and one as a gift for their mom, sister, or auntie. And if those other ladies need more supplies, they can come speak with you about it and buy them at a low cost from the seamstresses."*

Esther immediately responded that she thought it would work well. She left to go find 1,000 pair of underwear. Amazingly, that didn't take very long. So our program was back on track.

I didn't realize it at the time, but our 503 purses was almost the exact number we needed to give one purse to each girl, and an additional purse to their older sister, auntie, or mom. Coincidence? I started to think not.

The Miraculous Soap Man

That night we went on a shopping adventure for multi-purpose soap. We needed 500 bars and we had no idea how we were going to get them. If our purse distribution was going to happen that week, we had to solve the problem really quickly.

We walked into the grocery store near our hotel and looked at the soap aisle. It was fairly late and there was a man standing there in a brightly colored polo shirt. He was stocking the shelves and he could tell we didn't exactly know what we were looking for.

He said, *"Hello. What is it that you are looking for?"*

We said, *"Multi-purpose soap for hand washing clothes."*

Reaching for a specific bar of soap he said, *"Oh, you want this type."*

I noticed that there were only eight or ten bars of that type on the shelf. I said, *"Thanks, are you the store manager?"*

"No, I'm the regional Unilever sales representative and I come and do soap inventory at all the stores, and bring them what they need from our distribution center."

Bingo!

"Wow!" I said, *"So if we need 500 bars of this type by tomorrow morning do you think you could get them for me?"*

He had a shocked look on his face, but said, *"Sure. We'd be happy to help."*

Within a few minutes we had coordinated with him and the store manager. Both were very nice and helpful. At 9:00 am when the store opened we'd have our 500 bars of soap. Cost per bar, 58 cents.

We walked out of that store scratching our heads, completely convinced that another miracle had taken place. That soap man was another godsend. It seemed God had a lot of people he was starting to send.

Hey Unilever people, if you ever read this book—thank you for being helpful to us that night. We are truly grateful!

But How Much Does All This Cost?

Later that night in the hotel I worked on the expense side of our new project. Our Sew Powerful Purse was going to officially include:

- ✓ Two Shields
- ✓ Eight Liners
- ✓ Two pair of underwear
- ✓ A bar of soap
- ✓ And of course, the hand-written note card

We also needed to factor in the pay for seamstresses. For that we had already discussed how best to approach the work with Esther and the seamstresses. We settled on a piecework approach, which they proposed. They'd be paid based on completing a set of one shield and four liners. We wanted to make sure they felt like they were getting a good deal.

Cinnamon was sitting next to me as I was working on my laptop. At one point she said, *"So how much does it cost to supply each girl?"*

I said, "$4.93."

Our First Purse Distribution

On Thursday, June 4th, 2015, the day finally arrived when the health training was going to happen and we'd have our first Sew Powerful Purse distribution to girls. Our team scrambled that morning to put all the items into the purses. We were all nervous to see how it would go.

But first we had an important distribution to conduct. We went into the sewing room and asked the ladies to take a break for a few minutes. We gathered around in a big circle and thanked them for their enthusiasm and hard work. Then we told them that we felt like they should be the first to receive a purse and the supplies and asked them to pick out a purse. Dancing ensued! It was an amazing moment of camaraderie and shared effort.

After lunch, we set up for the health class. We were all nervous as the girls started to pour into the room. As it began, I did my best to stay out of the way and watch from the back so the girls wouldn't feel weird about it. Esther spoke to them for about thirty minutes. Most of the time it was in the local language, Nyanja, with English sprinkled in. They all learn and know English, but Nyanja is their local language.

During her talk she asked a question that I think was for our information more than hers, *"How many of you have 5 pair of underwear?"*

Two or three girls raised their hands.

"How many of you have 4 pairs of underwear?"

A few more girls raised their hand.

"How many of you have 3 pairs of underwear?"

A large group raised their hand.

"How many of you have 2 pairs of underwear?"

A third of the room raised their hand.

"How many of you have 1 pair of underwear?"

A third of the room raised their hand.

Then she turned to Cinnamon and said, *"Okay, now you can explain the pads."* The look on Cinnamon's face was priceless. She was not ready for that! But she stepped up and explained the pads and holders like she had done with the seamstresses. The girls clapped, cheered, and laughed.

Then Esther asked them if they had questions. The first question was, *"If my sister or auntie wants to buy more of this, how much does it cost?"* Wow. We were excited by that question—again, a great sign that the product was valuable. We had already worked out that the seamstresses could make a small clutch purse and use it when they were going to make pads and holders that they would sell locally.

Then Esther led them in the Sew Powerful Promise. She had them stand and asked them if they promised to come to school even when they are on their period.

"Yes!", they all shouted.

Then the girls went up, one by one, and were handed a purse. Cinnamon, Karen and Melinda got to distribute purses that they had made. Meeting the girls made the whole experience personal, meaningful, and deeply rewarding.

Then Esther explained the note cards — how the purse maker had written a special message inside the purse. We expected these to be a meaningful part of the project, but we were surprised how much it meant to the girls. They would carefully take out the card, read it, then turn to their friend and read it out loud to them. Then they'd thoughtfully look at the note, and carefully place it back into the purse.

We were reminded in that moment that they are mostly orphan girls, struggling to survive, many of them HIV Positive. The encouragement on those cards cut deeper than you might expect.

Time to Scale Up

We returned from that trip energized and convinced that our new strategy had merit and could really work at a larger scale. Oddly enough, we had a new problem to solve. We needed more girls. We had a feeling the purse makers were just getting started and the Zambian seamstresses could scale up their side of the program to a much larger number. Fortunately, I had a good idea of how we could solve this latest challenge.

Figure 8.1 *Celebrating together*

Figure 8.2 *The note cards are a very special part*

The Major Donors of Ngombe

By Jason

On July 16th, 2015, one of our board members, Dana Buck, set up an informational meeting for us at World Vision to discuss the project. The buzz was that we had set up a program that was fairly innovative and people at World Vision wanted to know more about it.

Specifically, there was a group at World Vision that was very interested in the topic of Menstrual Hygiene Management, the formal name for this type of program. In the non-profit sector this topic falls under the broader topic of Water And Sanitation Hygiene (WASH). The meeting included half a dozen managers and directors, many of them people I had worked with for many years, so it was a fun time. It also included the leaders of their Gift-In-Kind container shipping program.

We discussed a simple plan that we hoped would feel like a true all-around win for everyone involved. Here is how it would work:

- ✓ World Vision would ship the purses to Zambia through their container system of regularly sent Gift-In-Kind donations.

- ✓ The seamstresses at Needs Care would make the pads and holders, add the soap and underwear, and put it all together.

- ✓ Then Needs Care would donate the purses back to World Vision for distribution at World Vision program locations.

✓ World Vision would conduct the health training and work with the teachers.

✓ The girls would take the Sew Powerful Pledge.

✓ World Vision would document the attendance rates, monitor, and evaluate the program.

✓ Of course, all the girls at Needs Care would still receive purses first and that would always be our primary Zambian program location.

The team agreed, as long as the World Vision Zambia team would also agree to support the program as the key distribution partner. My friend Chikondi came to my mind immediately.

The most obvious benefit to this arrangement was that World Vision could ship an unlimited number of purses. They ship over 50 cargo containers per year to Zambia, so there is always one headed out.

Another fantastic benefit is that as the largest charity in Zambia, they work with more than 120,000 children. This program fits within their Water And Sanitation Hygiene (WASH) program goals; so with their help, we can scale distribution to a massive number as quickly as we're able.

Of course it also solves our challenge of finding girls that need the Sew Powerful purse—meaning we can scale up our efforts as aggressively as possible.

The Major Donors of Ngombe

But a much more interesting benefit of this arrangement is that we have effectively turned the seamstresses of Ngombe into major donors to World Vision Zambia. Let me explain this point a bit further, because it's a big deal and it speaks to the strength of our program model.

For record-keeping purposes, we decided to value each purse when filled with all the items at $25. So 1,000 purses would be valued by World Vision as a $25,000 donation. This is called a "Gift-In-Kind" product donation.

Of course the seamstresses in Ngombe haven't purchased the items. But they work hard to make it all happen and serve as the final assembly team. In our view, if there is anyone who deserves to be the hero of our story, we truly believe it's the seamstresses. They started as a group of moms trying to make jewelry to raise money for their desperate school, and took the time to learn to sew with the hope of it being a good trade skill. They've come a long way, and so has the school.

To think that they can scale their work to such a degree that it impacts tens of thousands of girls is remarkable. And regardless of whether they personally do that in the future, or our model is copied by other charities—either way, their hard work and willingness to make purposeful products a reality is the cornerstone of the whole idea.

A Farm Fresh Miracle

As we were leaving the meeting at World Vision, we received an amazing offer. We call it our Farm Fresh Miracle. David Derr is a Senior Director at World Vision and someone I've known for almost twenty years. He came up to us and casually said, *"I don't know if it would be of help to Esther, but my wife and I own 10 acres of farmland just outside of Lusaka. We bought it eight years ago, have always wanted to do something with it, and haven't known what to do. Maybe we can use it to grow food for the children at Needs Care."*

Cinnamon and I both stood there in stunned surprise. Then we both started laughing—it was such a random and unexpected idea. We were in shock! But in that moment we saw a vivid future in which our school lunch problem would be solved in an amazing way. Did God really just provide a 10-acre farm that could be dedicated to feeding the hungry kids at Needs Care?

We asked David how he had a farm in Zambia. He explained that eight years earlier, he and his wife Martha had decided to adopt two children from Zambia—Esther and Ivan. During the process, they also decided to purchase some property, so that in the future, if the children ever wanted to return to Zambia, they'd have a place to go.

The attorney that was organizing the adoption knew of a local farm owner that was selling 10-acre parcels of a once very large farm. David and Martha purchased the 10 acres, and it had been unused ever since. We told David we would discuss it with Esther and left with a huge smile on our faces.

I discussed the idea with Esther, and she was as shocked as we were. She was thrilled at the idea. We all started believing that David and Martha had purchased that land for just this purpose; the phrase from the book of Esther, verse 4:14, *"for such a time as this"*, came to our mind.

We began working on a plan. On August 8th we had a long-term formal agreement signed that gifted the 10 acres for the purpose of feeding the children at Needs Care.

That weekend I received a message from a stranger on Facebook. She asked if we could speak on the phone about our sewing program. As it turns out, she and her husband used to be missionaries in Lusaka, and had a heart for Ngombe Compound, as well as sewing. She was so excited about what we were doing that she funded the first project, the installation of a well on the property. Godsend! It was the first step in turning it into a real farm. This confirmed for us that we were on the right track.

Nicholas and Lillian Join the Team

Esther is not a farmer. But she was incredibly enthusiastic about this opportunity. So she drove to the property to see where it was located, what it looked like, and how it could begin to be used.

As she stood looking at the land, a neighbor from across the road walked over and introduced himself. His name was Nicholas. As you might guess, he was curious about what she was doing, so she told him the story. He was incredibly helpful, explained the location of various farms, who owned what property, what grew best, and the general details about the location.

Nicholas lived in a small house across the road with his wife and six children. His oldest daughter was married, and she and her husband, with their two children, also lived with them in the small house. Nicholas was a farm hand for the property owner who owned a large parcel on the other side of the road. He worked full-time in exchange for free rent. Unfortunately, that didn't allow him any money to send his younger children to school, so they didn't attend.

Over the next few weeks, as Esther would visit, Nicholas proved to be another Godsend. He was a twenty-year farm veteran and knew a huge amount about raising crops and livestock. But more than that, he was honest, hard working, and a wonderful guy. He helped her at every step. When she needed oxen to plow the field, he knew exactly who to borrow them from. When the materials for the new house arrived, he and his son-in-law slept outside next to them to make sure they wouldn't be stolen in the night.

As the caretaker's house was being completed, Esther had a brilliant idea. Maybe it was time for Nicholas to become a farm manager, get a new house, and take on more responsibilities. She proposed the idea to him, and he discussed it with his family. In addition to free rent, our offer included a monthly stipend, which would allow him to send his children to school.

Nicholas and Lillian accepted the offer and made new arrangements with their former employer. Their daughter and son-in-law would stay in the old house, in exchange for ongoing work on that farm. Nicholas and Lillian would live in the new house just across the road. Their children all enrolled in school—and we had a new farm manager.

The 3 Esthers Farm Is Born

As we brainstormed together, we settled on the name, The 3 Esthers Farm. There was Esther MKandawire in Ngombe; Esther Derr, the Zambian daughter of David and Martha; and the third Esther in reference to the scripture verse found in Esther 4:14: *"And who knows but that you have come to your royal position for such a time as this."*

In October we created a Crowd Funding project to raise money to launch the farm. Our goal was $10,000. By December, we had our funding. Esther had planned a budget that would allow us to build a caretaker's house, fence the property, drill a well, and begin setting up crops and animal projects. The 3 Esthers Farm was off to a great start.

Going Global

During 2015 we also launched an improved purse pattern. People from around the world began advocating the program. We could feel that the program was beginning to extend beyond our original Liberty Jane customer base. We did our best to blog and tell the story, and people started to get excited about participating.

This global enthusiasm was typified by an email we received on July 3rd, 2015, that blew our minds. Someone from Australia named Kylie Gersekowski said: *"Hi, I just read about your wonderful charity and would love to help. I am pulling together a heap of lovely sewing ladies on Facebook to see if we can sew a number of these purses and send them to you from all over the world. I just thought I would let you know, as I may need some more detail in the future."*

Australia? How in the world did our program get popular in Australia? We had no idea. Or maybe we did—Kylie! We thanked her, introduced ourselves, and began making new friends in her Facebook group. That group now has over 800 people in it. You can join it at:

https://www.facebook.com/groups/sewpowerfulpurseproject/

The seemingly spontaneous appearance of take-charge leaders who organized groups of seamstresses in places like India, New Zealand, and the U.K. made the program feel like a movement.

I'll never forget seeing an advertisement for one Sew Powerful purse-making event in the U.K. It announced their keynote speaker as a lady from Sew Powerful that we had never heard of before. We had no idea if she knew anything about our program, but we didn't mind. We thought it was amazing.

We also started asking purse makers to consider donating $5 for each purse they make to help cover the cost of the contents. This was a suggestion, not a requirement, and we truly believed that with the help of some generous purse makers, we could cover the new program expenses.

Going Postal

Because we immediately had purse makers ask if they could continue to send us purses, we quickly developed our "Priority Deadline" strategy. We are happy to accept purses all year long, but consider October 1st and February 1st as our two priority deadlines. That seems to work well.

During a conversation with our board, we explained our post office problem. One of our board members, Kevin LaRoche, who serves as the Youth Pastor at our church, offered to have the packages all start coming to the church instead. They could be sent to Cally, the Youth Administrator, and then Cinnamon and I could collect them each week.

Within a few months Kevin reported back that the Renton Post office was unhappy. The volume of packages was not customary, the Postmaster didn't like it, and it was going to be a problem.

But a few weeks later, a funny thing happened. Kevin reported back that he and Cally had taken the time to discuss the project with the mail lady. They explained the sewing cooperative in Zambia, the desperate situation in Ngombe, how the girls don't go to school when they are on their period, and how this program can really help change their lives. Surprisingly, the whole thing turned around. The mail lady became an advocate for our program. Problem solved.

Our 2nd Unboxing Party—Livestreamed

Our October 2015 Priority Deadline quickly came, and we had a lot of boxes that had piled up; but we had no idea how many purses we had. It was time to find out.

We decided to expand our unboxing party idea from the previous year, and invited our entire church youth group to help us.

So on November 8th, 2015, we worked to unbox purses, count them, make sure they had a note card inside, and prepare them to be shipped to Zambia. I took the time to explain the program to everyone there, and make sure they understood the importance of what we were doing.

Kevin and Cally even invited the Renton Post Office mail lady. She came and had a great time helping us.

We also decided at the last minute to livestream the party and invite purse makers to watch it live over the Internet. It turned out to be one of the most fun aspects of the night.

People from around the world watched as our board members Toby Capps and Kevin LaRoche held up each package and read the name and location of the purse maker. People loved it. A new annual tradition was born.

At the end of the night we had collected 1,619 purses. We were thrilled at the outcome. We had tripled the number of purses from the prior year. And as with the prior year, those purses were shipped to Zambia and they arrived just in time for our 2016 trip.

Mom-Approved Goals

By Jason

A nother amazing thing started to happen during 2015. More and more people asked if they could go with us to Zambia to see the program. We now have a waiting list, and people regularly ask us if there is space. You can join it here if you're interested:

http://www.sewpowerful.org/trips

Our Summer 2016 Visit

In July 2016, Cinnamon and I led our largest group yet—fourteen of us went to visit the seamstresses, school, and 3 Esthers Farm. The group included five purse makers that were excited to see the program, as well as people with a passion for healthcare and education.

As in prior years, the children, teachers, and seamstresses greeted us with singing and dancing. This year, during the welcoming ceremony, they asked us to sing them a song. With absolutely no prior planning, we were on the spot. Jesus Loves Me came to mind and we all sang it as loud as we could.

Then Esther asked us to jump right in and help serve the children their lunch. It was one scoop of porridge per child. The group members took turns serving the children. After having seen this same daily ritual for the last three years, I had grown to hate it—not because of what it was, a bit of food; but because of what it wasn't. It wasn't enough food. It wasn't good food. If they were our children, and this was our children's school, we would do anything on earth to make it better.

New Sewing Tools

The Zambian seamstresses had the sewing of the pads and holders down to a science. But our team included veteran quilt makers and seamstresses. They watched the process, and then introduced several new sewing and construction techniques. Their recommendations helped save both time and material. The Zambian seamstresses were excited to learn the new techniques. They are very aware that the faster they can make the items, the more money they make.

We also brought and introduced a new set of tools in the sewing room— KAM Snaps, which improved the construction of the holder portion of the product. The seamstresses were excited about that product upgrade.

Prior to our arrival, the seamstresses had been busy too. There were huge bags of pads and holders nicely counted and ready to be placed in the purses. The 1,619 purses had arrived in Zambia a few weeks before, and were already at Needs Care.

Expanding Beyond Needs Care

On the third day of our trip, we went to visit an old friend, Chikondi Phiri, The Deputy National Director of World Vision Zambia. It was time to work out the details of the Purse donation. The Needs Care School would use 400 of the purses for their program, which left 1,219 purses that could be distributed to girls via the World Vision program.

Chikondi warmly welcomed us, gave us a tour of the facility, explained the size and scope of their program, and then shared how the Sew Powerful Purse program fit so nicely into their Water Sanitation And Hygiene (WASH) program goals.

We let him know that the Sew Powerful seamstresses in Ngombe had 1,200 purses being filled with all the supplies, which we would be donating. He was thrilled, not just because it was a great donation, but truly in awe that it was coming from a ministry partner in Ngombe Compound. This was not something that had ever happened before.

He explained that they had a program site called One Chongwe that was just 45 minutes away, and that his team was excited about the opportunity to introduce the purse program to the schoolgirls there. It was a more rural area, and the girls were dealing with the same challenges; our purse program was desperately needed.

I was excited when he mentioned the One Chongwe location because I had been there before, in 2009, and was familiar with the location and communities.

I told him that we really felt that our program was just getting started, and that we'd be thrilled to have One Chongwe as our second program location. Our hope was that in 2017 we'd have even more purses for them.

I asked him how many purses he would need if he were going to replicate our model and provide two purses for each girl, like we did in Ngombe. He said yes, we want to replicate what you've done; we need 5,000 purses.

As he said the words *"five thousand,"* my eyes quickly scanned the room. I tried to see the look on the faces of our purse makers. I instantly wondered if I would see dread or enthusiasm. What I saw was a mix of pleasant surprise, enthusiasm, and instant determination. After the nervous laughter and "wow" comments died down, I said *"Well, it looks like we have a new goal for 2017."*

Fun Farm Math

The next day we were off to visit the 3 Esthers Farm. We were able to walk the property, see the progress, and meet Nicholas, Lillian and their family. The progress on the farm exceeded our hopes and expectations. You can see updates and learn more at www.3esthersfarm.org.

As I prepared our group agenda for the trip, I tried to figure out what 14 of us could do during an entire day-long visit to the farm. Then I hit on a pretty good idea. We stopped on the way, purchased 10 orange trees, as well as several other fruit trees, and as a group we planted them. Nicholas was thrilled with the idea. He picked the spots and had even pre-dug the holes. He told us that the 3-foot high trees would begin producing oranges within a year.

A local orange grower told us that once mature, the variety we planted would produce 3,000 oranges on average, per tree, per year. Wow—that seems like a lot of oranges!

As we stood there, I could just imagine the ten trees producing 30,000 oranges a year—and then being delivered to the children at Needs Care. Delicious, big, vitamin packed oranges! That ought to help!

But then I did the math as my mind continued to explore the idea. One orange per day for 1,400 children ... times...five days a week ... times... 43.3 weeks (ten months) equals 303,100 oranges per year. I had to use my IPhone calculator to help with the math.

So we simply needed 100 fully mature orange trees to make that happen. We already had ten trees that we just planted, so we just needed 90 more trees. Each tree cost $4.30 cents, so that's only $387. That seemed easy.

But then Nicholas said, *"Okay, now we have to water the trees."*

Figure 10.1 *Nicholas explaining farm details*

The trees are roughly 75 yards away from the newly installed hand-pumped well. It's a 150-yard round trip from the well to the trees. So you walk to the well, pump the handle until water starts flowing, then fill the bucket, walk to the tree, water it, and repeat to do the second tree.

We had just created fourteen 150-yard daily laps for Nicholas, not including the energy used in pumping the well handle and carrying the bucket. Of course, as the trees grow, they won't need water every day; but as the oranges and other fruit trees actually start to mature and require picking, packing, and delivery to the school, the work will multiply.

3 Esthers Farm Phase Two

As we sat under a nice shade hut as a group and ate our packed lunches, we discussed the potential of the farm, the next steps, and the challenges we saw. We were all amazed at what had been accomplished, incredibly impressed with Nicholas, and excited about the potential impact on Needs Care. Clearly we needed a second fundraising campaign so we could complete a new set of items on the farm.

Our first fundraiser had allowed us to complete the caretaker's house, the borehole well and hand pump, fencing around the entire property, several smaller structures, some goats, and a 2-acre soybean crop that had already been harvested.

Phase Two would help us deliver a new set of projects including:

✓ Electricity being run to the farm by the regional utility company

✓ Wiring the caretaker's house

✓ All the equipment needed to transform our hand-pumped well into a complete watering system, including a metal tower, large water tank, electric water pump and all the pipes and hoses to enable a better watering system

✓ A barn for a large chicken project

✓ More farm hands to expand production

It's obvious that the farm has huge potential to help feed the children of Needs Care, improve the quality of the school program, and employ people; but as with most things, it's a long-term project.

The Needs Care Clinic

Because we had several nurses in our group as well as others that had a background in the medical industry, the team wanted to know more details about the clinic. It was a learning experience for all of us.

The clinic is funded by a couple in Seattle that Cinnamon and I had met in 2012. He is a Doctor and she is a nurse. The clinic operates in a small house across the street from the Needs Care School and is open two days a week.

If the clinic is going to assist the children in a more comprehensive way, then we need to raise more funds, expand the program, and establish it more formally.

The Teachers of Needs Care

The 2016 trip was also different in another way. This group included a family with four kids under fifteen. So we worked before the trip to come up with some interesting ways they could participate in the trip. We settled on origami, a passion of theirs, and something the children at Needs Care had never seen before.

For several days we spent more time with the teachers at Needs Care. There are eight teachers, and they do double shifts: they teach two entirely different groups of students—one in the morning, one in the afternoon.

On the last day, I asked Esther if I could leave the school, walk down to the garbage-filled ravine, and take a few pictures. She asked one of the teachers to go with me. As we walked, I began asking questions.

"Why do you teach at Needs Care?"

"Well, we have a heart for the children here and want to see them have a better life."

"How long have you taught here?"

"This is my third year now."

"How much is your salary on a monthly basis?"

"1,000 Kwacha" (which is $100).

"Is the pay you receive at Needs Care equal to what you would receive at a school outside Ngombe?"

"No, at other schools, teachers might make closer to $2,500 Kwacha" ($250 a month).

We got to the ravine, and as I stood on the bridge, I turned on my video camera and took video in both directions. I hadn't counted on the intense odor. Wow! So I got the video clip, turned off the camera and we walked back and continued our conversation.

I asked these questions to learn more, but I already had a pretty good understanding of the situation at the school. Esther has a very hard time keeping teachers because of both the pay she can provide as well as the challenges of the environment. If the school is going to be improved, it will need more donors.

Esther's Vision

On our last day in Lusaka, we had lunch with Esther. The group asked her questions about various aspects of the ministry. Someone asked, *"Esther, what's your vision, what's your priority?"*

Her answer was *"If we keep the girls in school with the purse program, and they pass their 7th grade exam, but we fail to help them complete Secondary School, then we've left them half way. We need to expand the school and offer a full Secondary School program in Ngombe."*

I asked, *"What percentage of your students go on to Secondary School right now?"*

She said, *"Maybe 25% at the most."*

The conversation continued and we discussed hopes and dreams for the clinic, farm, and sewing program. Our group left in awe of Esther's commitment, determination, and humility.

Our Mom-Approved Goals

I left Lusaka very troubled. It was very clear that the mission and vision of Sew Powerful were expanding. We had a farm, which was a miracle. But we obviously needed to raise awareness and funding for the school and clinic too. Things were expanding beyond sewing. Should we let them? Cinnamon and I discussed the obvious implications.

- ✓ If we expand to raise funds and awareness for these additional needs, are the purse makers going to be confused?
- ✓ Is "Sew Powerful" even the right name for our charity if we are going to focus on an expanded set of topics?
- ✓ How do we weave it all together?
- ✓ Should we ignore these other topics and leave them for someone else to help with?

For the next few weeks, we pondered what to do. It was time to do soul searching and clarify what we were going to do. One thing that comforted me was the realization that our group of 12 travelers had absolutely no issue integrating it all as we talked about it. The reasons for the clinic and farm were so compelling; there was no question in their minds that we needed to focus on those areas in addition to the sewing cooperative and purse program.

We returned from Zambia and met with our Board of Directors. It was a fun night of sharing, celebrating the success of the program, and planning for the future. Preparing for the meeting gave me an added sense of urgency to clarify our thoughts and plans.

By the day of our board meeting, I had found peace in a simple way. I took a journey in my mind back to 2009. I looked again at the pictures, reflected on what I had seen, and remembered things I had forgotten over the years.

What I began to realize was that the moms of Needs Care were on their own mission that day in March 2009. I remembered the dancing and clapping I had heard as we bought all their handmade jewelry. I began looking at it from their point of view. They had accomplished a lot in the seven years, but there was still more to do.

Their passion was making money so they could make the school a better place. That was their mission. They didn't even know anything about sewing at that point. A sewing program was never the original goal. The income from the sewing was, and still is, a means to an end. The end goal was to improve the school and have it be a vibrant place for the children of Ngombe.

With this clarity, my new role was clear: tell their story to a larger audience, share in their goals, and help raise money for the key elements including:

- ✓ Education: teacher salaries, school improvements, janitorial and maintenance people, supplies, and eventually an expansion into a full Secondary School campus

- ✓ Food: delivering as much farm-fresh nutritious food as we possibly can to the school children

- ✓ Health: ensure the clinic is expanded so the children get excellent medical support

Our sewing program is making a difference in Ngombe and beyond. But it would be wrong if the sewing work didn't fulfill the mission the moms originally had.

If our sewing program doesn't transform the school in a vibrant way and change the lives of the children, our model just isn't complete. Can sewing be powerful enough to do it?

Telling the Full Story

The night of the Board meeting came, and we had a great conversation about these topics. The Board was in unanimous agreement that we should begin telling the full story, raising funds for the school, the clinic, and the farm, in addition to the sewing program. These other topics would simply be on-going special projects.

When I expressed my concern about the name of our program being Sew Powerful, but the topics being much broader, one of our board members put it very nicely:

"Sewing purses engages your audience in a way that is amazing. It includes them in the mission and purpose in a way that they enjoy and is incredibly helpful. Once they're engaged, tell them the whole story. They'll want to get involved and do more."

A Vision for The Future

As we left that night, we began to dream of our expanded plans:

- ✓ We want to continue to grow the sewing cooperative and have a bigger space, more seamstresses, and reach more children across Zambia, particularly girls via the Sew Powerful Purse program.
- ✓ We want the school to be a vibrant place of learning with engaged teachers, supplies, and a facility that is safe and effective.
- ✓ We want to see the 3 Esthers Farm produce a maximum amount of food for the school lunches, and be a terrific location for school field trips and various training activities.
- ✓ We want the clinic to expand to ensure each student has good care so their lifespan is not compromised due to HIV or related illnesses.

We Are Sew Powerful—Fundraisers

In the upcoming chapters, we are going to share ways you can join us as we do our best to tell the story of the moms of Ngombe, Needs Care, and the Sew Powerful program. Making purses is a huge gift and serves as the centerpiece of our entire program. But there are other simple things that can be done and we hope you'll take the time to consider getting involved in one or two of them.

But first, we want to share your stories...

PART FOUR

Your Stories

"After nourishment, shelter and companionship, stories are the thing we need most in the world."

—Phillip Pullman

Section Introduction

By Jason & Cinnamon

Our journey with Sew Powerful had felt like a very lonely effort for most of the last seven years. We frequently found ourselves trying to tell people about Ngombe and Needs Care, hoping they'll want to get involved, only to have them politely smile, and change the topic. They don't get it.

On occasion, someone would give a gift, comment in a supportive way, or extend their support. It always felt like a godsend. It always made us smile, put a skip in our step, and reminded us that we are not alone in this work.

Then in 2014, with the launch of our Board of Directors, and the Sew Powerful Purse, the feelings of togetherness blossomed. Each day, whether we receive a purse in the mail, got a financial gift, or a new friend on social media, we are reminded we are not alone in this important work. God was sending a lot of people who got the vision. We began to build a growing group of partners who care for these orphans and widows like we do.

So as we developed the idea for this book, we asked you to send us your Sew Powerful stories, and we were blown away by what we received. We hope this section inspires you like it inspires us.

The Power of A Purse

By Jan Paul

Fayetteville, Arkansas

*C*an a purse be powerful? Interesting question. It reminds me of those old TV shows where the little old lady whacks a guy over the head with her purse. Recently God showed me the power of a purse without actually hitting me over the head, but He did get my attention!

I initially heard about Sew Powerful's Purse Project in 2014. I downloaded the pattern, looked over the instructions, got confused and gave up! Wow, THAT'S an inspiring story, isn't it? Pitiful!

However, since I'd requested a pattern, I continued to get updates on the program. As I followed the Sew Powerful story, I became more and more interested in what was happening half a world away at the Needs Care School in Zambia. God was growing a love in me for these children who lived in one of the world's poorest urban slums.

I read and reread the 2014 trip reports and updates on Sew Powerful's website. According to data collected, these purses were certainly powerful in the lives of the girls. Because of a purse, not only were girls missing fewer days of school at Needs Care, but they also had a much better shot at passing an exam to continue their education—and, ultimately, improve their lives. I was very disappointed I hadn't participated.

Fast forward to me getting an email in July about the new 2015 purse pattern—of course, I rushed immediately to download that pattern and start sewing purses like my machine was on fire! Um…not.

Sadly, once again I had the best of intentions...I wanted to make a purse, but when I finally downloaded the pattern in September, the directions still seemed daunting, even though I've been sewing for years. Then I got an email from Sew Powerful about an instructional video! (Cue heavenly organ music and beams of light breaking through clouds!)

I watched that video over and over, found some cute fabric in my stockpile and, finally cut out a purse! I sewed with my iPad right beside my machine, step-by-step, rewinding and re-watching each step until I got it right. Oh, and yes, there was frequent use of the seam ripper! But one purse was finished! Hallelujah!

But wait, hadn't one of the emails said Jason and Cinnamon were praying, asking and expecting 1000 purses for this year? And they were asking for this incredible number when they barely got 500 the previous year? I confess I doubted that prayer would be answered. So, I got busy making more purses, as if it somehow depended on me.

At about this time I found out about a Facebook page started by some wonderful Australian seamstresses who were sharing information and encouragement with other purse makers. Posting pictures of finished purses and receiving compliments from others who were working toward the same goal was incredibly motivating! We were a team!

The girls for whom we sewed became "our girls." As I followed the sewing progress via social media, it started to dawn on me how many purses were being made literally all around the world: Australia, India, Britain, Canada, New Zealand, and the U.S. Some precious lady in South Carolina had made over *fifty* purses, and was still going!

Jason sent updates about the *wall* of boxes that was stacking up as purses began to arrive. Still in the back of my mind I questioned whether the goal would be met. I sewed as many purses as I could by the November 11th "extension," and sent them off.

On the night of the "unboxing," my husband and I excitedly watched the live stream to see if we could spot the boxes I'd mailed. (We did!) When we heard someone say on the video that they had to go out and buy more plastic bags, we looked at each other, "Surely that means they have over a thousand purses!" When the totals started being announced, it was quite obvious the goal would be met! I thanked God for answered prayer and headed to bed.

When I got up the next day and looked online for the final count, I was stunned! 1,619 purses! God had provided far over and above what was asked for or expected! His portion to those precious girls wasn't just a full cup, but an overflowing one! Why had I doubted? What had made me think my pitiful efforts were even necessary?

Today, as I think about the scope of the Sew Powerful project, God's goodness in allowing me to play even a small part in it is humbling—kind of like being whacked over the head with an old lady's purse. Powerfully humbling! I thought I was sewing purses to make a difference in the lives of the girls—and I was, but as it turns out, God had me sewing purses to cause a change in my heart as well. He was patiently growing my faith, allowing me to see a glimpse of how big He really is!

So back to the question: Can a purse be powerful? Well, let's see....

✓ God is using a purse to improve the lives of girls living in extreme poverty by providing greater educational opportunities for them.

✓ He's using a purse to build a worldwide community of seamstresses with the common goal of showing these girls how very much they are loved and valued.

✓ And He's using a purse to continue to teach me much-needed lessons about His faithfulness and sovereignty.

Yep. I'd say that's one powerful purse!

A Passion for Africa

By Shirley Utz
Houston, Texas

Sew Powerful has really been about answered prayer for me. When I was a young girl, God laid a passion for Africa on my heart. In 2007 I traveled to Tanzania as part of mission team. That only increased my passion for Africa. So at the beginning of 2015, I asked God to let me return to Africa, and also to help me use my sewing skills to do something worthwhile.

I'm retired. I love to sew, although, I am not a professional seamstress. I love shopping for fabric but really need to make very little for myself or my family. I head a group at my church that sews for the local pregnancy center and for nursing homes, but I needed something that really struck a chord in my heart.

And then I saw a posting about Sew Powerful on Facebook and took a look at the page—it was perfect! Africa… sewing…fabric…the possibility of returning to the continent I've been in love with most of my life.

I bought fabric to make purses, and then I wound up with a severe eye infection, making sewing purses nearly impossible. I dreamed of purses and the girls who would receive them. I dreamed of lives changed by the opportunity for education. I dreamed of sewing the purses I'd bought the fabric to make. And eventually I was able to do that; it wasn't as many as I'd hoped to make, but I had latched on to the dream.

I've applied to go on the 2016 trip to Zambia and see firsthand what Sew Powerful is accomplishing through its cooperation with the Needs Care Centre in Lusaka. My heart is full.

But there's more—today I had lunch at a local restaurant I love. It's owned and operated by a wonderful Christian family. The restaurant is raising funds to help support orphan girls in a town in India. Joanne and I began talking about that, and then I told her about my sewing adventure with Sew Powerful. She mentioned how she'd love for her home-schooled girls to learn to sew, but she doesn't know how. I offered to teach them, and…well…she wants her girls to reach a point where they, too, can sew purses for girls in Zambia. My heart is fuller still!

I knew from the moment I saw the Sew Powerful website, that God's hand was on the ministry. And now He's orchestrating some new things, not just for Sew Powerful, but for me, personally, through that same ministry. Did I mention that my heart is full?

Follow Up—My Trip to Ngombe

GOD continues to answer prayer. I was part of the team that went to Zambia in July 2016!

The trip for my team was originally scheduled to depart on May 14th; but, due to illnesses, that trip was cancelled and a couple of us were transferred to the July team. Even though my heart was set on going in May, this turned out to be best, because my mother-in-law died shortly before the originally scheduled trip; I would not have been able to go. GOD had everything orchestrated down to the last detail.

We were each able to bring a suitcase filled with sewing and educational supplies for the seamstresses and school teachers at the Needs Care School. In order to make my church more aware, I set up a Sign Up Genius page for contributions; everything from Gingher scissors to paperclips was on the list. It was so amazing to see how quickly people came forward with contributions. Those who didn't provide actual items, gave me cash. (That cash, along with some from a friend outside my congregation, purchased a Snap Press for the seamstresses.) Most of these donors did not sew, but this gave them an opportunity to participate in Sew Powerful and learn about it. One of those donors has become a "champion" for Sew Powerful at my church and also a dear friend.

The trip itself was incredible. Meeting the indomitable Esther; hearing the stories of the seamstresses who are now able to provide for their families and send their children to school; hearing the stories of the girls who received purses last year and the difference it made for them in attending school; seeing the smiling faces of girls as they received purses created by women around the world; seeing the difference a nearby clinic makes to the school and the community in the fight against AIDS; seeing the miracle of Three Esthers Farm and the hard work of another miracle named Nicholas; sharing all of this with a team of like-minded, extraordinary people, including four remarkable kids.

I was blessed beyond measure. I will continue to make purses and advocate for Sew Powerful because the memories of this trip are indelibly imprinted on my mind.

When I make a purse, I see a real person at the other end.

Entering Ngombe, there is what we would call a landfill. It was a deep gully filled with trash; but growing up the side of the gully was a very large blooming bougainvillea. The deep pink colors and beauty were a stark contrast to the garbage nearby. Flowers bloom in unlikely places. Hope is found in the darkest places. There is so much "darkness" in Ngombe: the extreme poverty, the AIDS epidemic, the weariness; but there is also great hope. That hope was reflected at the Needs Care School, in the Sewing Cooperative, at the Three Esthers Farm, at the clinic, and in the faith and determined spirit of a woman named Esther.

Our Burning Home

By Christina Porter
Ontario, Canada

hat comes to mind when you think of a seamstress who sews for charity? A nice, traditional lady who "gives back"? Well, that's not me.

I'm not sure I'm that nice, I'm certainly not traditional and the only time I've "given back" was when I re-gifted a bottle of wine back to my sister.

No, I am a career-minded, type A personality, President and General Manager at a global pharmaceutical company who travels on business a good part of the year; an insomniac, perfectionist and nag. Just ask my husband and daughters!

And I sew. I sew because my girls' dance costumes don't fit, and sewing takes my mind off of work. I sew because it reminds me of simpler times, and I like making things. I sew for me. I sew because I'm selfish.

Dec 16, 2014, 3:30 am: We awoke to the sound of a blaring smoke alarm and the screams of my eldest daughter. We ran out of our burning home, stood in a snow bank in bare feet and pajamas and thanked God we had all escaped. As we watched smoke pouring out of our windows and doors, we wondered where we would go and how we would start again.

I was surprised to find the things I missed the most in those early days after the fire were my sewing machine and fabric stash. I never could have imagined how much comfort my perfectly organized collection of threads, buttons and trims gave me.

So, I took the insurance money and replaced everything. I bought the best sewing machine. I replaced every bobbin, pin and scissor. I organized everything neatly in my new sewing basket. Then I stared at it all in dismay. There was no comfort in these new things.

Every spool I lost in the fire had a story. Every sequined piece of trim shone with hours and hours of dance practice, every scrap of fabric was a baby blanket or favorite sleeper, an Easter outfit, quilt or curtain. Every piece of lace, a graduation dress.

I was angry at our loss and feeling sorry for myself. And that's when God helped me to look at my new things with different eyes—as a stack of promise. What could this thread become? How could this sewing machine help to construct a better future?

I can't remember how, but He led me to Sew Powerful.

In the hazy days that followed our fire, I began to sew again. I sewed purses in every spare moment. I sewed instead of working late. I sewed instead of organizing, I sewed instead of nagging.

While I sewed, I thought about how much we take for granted. I meditated on the value of an education. I thought about all the opportunities available to me and my daughters. I thought about the girls who can't go to school...just because they are girls. I worked and prayed that these purses and this mission would change the future for girls in Zambia.

And for the first time, I sewed for someone else. For the first time, I gave away everything I made. I finally "gave back" for real, and I was at peace.

I'm still a Type A personality, my career is still important to me, and I'm still a perfectionist. But this year, I hope make a trip to Zambia for God instead of making yet another trip for business. I intend to continue to prayerfully sew purses, spread the word about Sew Powerful and hopefully become a little nicer and a little less selfish while I'm at it.

I Couldn't Stop Crying

By Dawn Carroll

Texas

I started sewing in 9th grade when my elderly neighbor, who had no children of her own, eagerly taught me everything she knew about sewing. I loved sewing! I loved the creativity and the challenge of problem solving when something did not work with either the sewing machine or pattern. I carried that skill that she passed on to me during my high school years by making my own clothes and mending other people's clothes.

In 1986, a month after our honeymoon, my husband and I went on an eight-week mission trip to Togo, West Africa. Our team leader asked me, since I knew how to sew, to come up with a craft that the African ladies could make to sell at their local market. I was delighted to be able to use my sewing skills in this way to honor the Lord. By the time our eight-week mission trip was over, my husband and I had fallen in love with the Togo people and did not want to go home. We hoped to return later as missionaries ourselves.

After returning back to America, I still had a burden for the Togolese people; but due to circumstances, my husband and I did not return to Africa like we had planned as missionaries. Through the years, I always had the desire to go back one day to Togo to serve, but did not know how or when that would be possible. I continued to use my sewing skills in various ways to bless other people from mending garments for people, to sewing gifts, sewing curtains and decorative items, to making costumes for a Shakespeare play and even teaching a beginner's sewing class. But I still had a longing to combine Africa and my sewing again.

Fast forward to 2015, and I had begun to seriously pray that somehow God would enable me to minister again to Africa with my sewing skills. I did not know how God was going to do it, because at the time I did not know any ministries connected to Africa. I decided I would have to just pray and wait on the Lord!

In September our family went to a business conference in Kentucky. I had no idea that the Lord was about to answer my prayers. When Jason and Cinnamon Miles presented their ministry with Sew Powerful, I knew the Lord had miraculously connected my sewing skills again with Africa! I could not stop crying. I was so overjoyed! I could not believe that the Lord had miraculously answered my prayer. Who would have ever dreamed that it was going to be through a business meeting that the Lord would answer?

When our family got home from the business trip, my daughter and I immediately began to get the details about making the purses for Sew Powerful. It is through Sew Powerful that I am so excited to be able to use my sewing skills to serve the Lord and Africa again! One day, I hope the Lord will miraculously answer my prayer to be able to go back to visit those African people that I realized the Lord had given me a love for back in 1986 on our mission trip; but until then, I will gladly support Sew Powerful!

We Arrived In Lusaka

By Kathy Simonsen
Ashland, Oregon

I am a retired empty nester who loves to sew and to sew with a purpose. It is very important to me to be creating something that someone can use or enjoy wearing. God has also given me a heart for women in developing countries.

When I heard about Sew Powerful, which combines two of my passions, I was in! I was impressed with the careful documentation of the project and its effects on the girls and women in the community in Zambia. If I was to be involved, it was very important to me that this project would actually meet a need.

I love how the women are earning a living by sewing the sanitary products and small purses. It is not just a handout or a project to make us westerners feel good. Of course, it is a perk that I know my sewing has a purpose by changing the life of a young girl, allowing her to continue with her education. It has also impressed me that Jason and Cinnamon began Sew Powerful because they wanted to serve God with their talents and skills. I am so thankful that I can be a small part of this great project.

It was with excitement and a little trepidation that I applied to go on the trip to Lusaka, Zambia, with Sew Powerful in July of 2016—excited, because I would be able to see the impact of the purses I had been sewing; and fearful, because I would be traveling with 13 people

I did not know to a country and culture that was unfamiliar. Through Facebook, I met the others on the team and knew I would be with like-minded travelers, who care for the underserved in a developing nation.

After flying for the longest time, we arrived in Lusaka. Esther and Matilda met us at the airport along with Jeffrey, our bus driver. As we were driving through the streets of this large capital city, I was impressed with the roads and sanity of the traffic.

The next morning, we traveled in our bus to Ngombe Compound. Here we saw the difference between the richer part of the city and one of the poorest slums. The streets were unpaved and full of potholes, some deep enough to wonder if the bus would remain upright. We passed a ravine that was obviously used as their dump. The streets were filled with young people and children. This area has been deeply affected by the AIDS epidemic; so many of the middle-aged have died from the disease.

Esther, the seamstresses, teachers and children, greeted us at Needs Care School. The morning was filled with the singing of the children followed by helping with the feeding of the students. Our team shared in the distribution of the porridge for each student. It was sobering to know that this is the only food some of them will receive each day.

The afternoon and the next morning were spent unpacking all the beautiful purses that had been made by seamstresses from all over the world. The purses were then filled with the washable sanitary pads, underwear and soap. The seamstresses and myself were honored to be able to hand out the purses that we had sewn. One girl, who had lost both parents to AIDS, commented that her grandmother would never be able to afford a purse this nice. Part of receiving the purses and supplies, was a promise by the girls to not miss a day of school because of their monthly period.

Later in the week, the team was able to talk to five of the girls who had received purses the year before. They all shared how well the pads worked and were able to stay in school all month. One girl had one complaint that the pads did not dry fast enough. She washes her own pads and hangs them to dry. With Esther's help interpreting, we discovered that she had been sharing pads from a friend and now with her new purse she would share some with her sister. We all agreed that she needed another purse for her sister! Jason encouraged her to tell her sister that we care for her and want her to also do well in school. Another girl, through tears, thanked us for the soap, as her mother cannot afford to buy soap.

I came away from this time with the girls knowing that sewing a few purses and donating a little money does make a difference. Together with Sew Powerful and all those sewing purses, and donating money for supplies, we can have a valuable effect on the lives of girls in Ngombe—not only to help them stay in school all month, but to give them encouragement by knowing that someone in another country cares for them. It also helps them have goals beyond getting married at an early age and having many children.

The team traveled to 3 Esthers Farm on Wednesday. The farm is 10 acres of land that will eventually grow food to feed the children in Ngombe at Needs Care School. It was a great privilege as part of the team to help plant ten orange trees, two guava trees and two avocado trees, that will eventually produce fruit for the sweet children at Needs Care School.

What a joy it was to meet the seamstresses, who have a room at the school set up with sewing machines! They spend their day sewing the washable sanitary pads out of flannel, along with the waterproof liners. They also make the school uniforms for the children, including using the knitting machine to knit all of their sweaters!

My small, regular donations are critical to help support the seamstresses. Because of the sewing cooperative, they have employment to help send their children to school, and to provide for some of their basic needs in an environment where there are not a lot of options. The money all goes to the ministry that is changing lives.

I left Lusaka being so impressed with Esther, a woman from the Ngombe Compound, who prayed for a school for the children and through the grace of God has accomplished that vision. The school has grown to seven grades in its own building and teaches and feeds the children. In addition, she has started a clinic that is staffed by a nurse that provides family planning to the women of the neighborhood, seeing 80–100 women each Tuesday.

Sew Powerful has come alongside Esther, a woman who knows the needs of her community, and started a ministry that provides financial help and vision to make it successful.

I feel more and more passionate about Sew Powerful. Jason and Cinnamon in their humility and care for the needy of Ngombe Compound have a beautiful model coming alongside a local school, supporting local seamstresses and letting the local leadership determine the best way to empower these children and women to rise above their circumstances with practical solutions.

I Let Out a Squeal

By Kylie Gersekowski

Pittsworth Queensland, Australia

About 12 months ago, while sitting outside in sunny Queensland in Australia, I stumbled upon the Sew Powerful Purse Project. I was looking for a charity sewing project, which linked my love of sewing bags with making a difference to someone else.

I remember when I was reading the Sew Powerful Purse Project purpose, I let out a squeal! Not only could I sew my favorite items, but I could make a difference to women from another country!

I have always had a passion for helping others, and have worked with people with disabilities and medical conditions for a long time. To help others even in a small way makes my heart sing.

I have a friend who is Zambian. She has told me many stories about her home country and the difficulties women in particular face, difficulties she faced as a young girl. I discussed the Sew Powerful Purses project with her and her face lit up—she could not believe there was such a project.

We talked about the bags specifically and she told me what a huge difference this would make to these girls. This just cemented the idea that this was something I wanted to be a part of, and not in a small way.

After making a few Sew Powerful Purses—and oh, what fun they were to sew—I started to wonder if other Aussie sewers might like to share my enthusiasm for this project. At this point, I started a Facebook group—and boy, did it grow fast! It began as a group for Aussies to sew purses, share their work, and encourage and support each other. This very quickly became a group for everyone, no matter where they were from, to share in this process.

This Facebook group became more than just another group. Friendships were formed, stories were told, encouragement and joy were shared between members on the completion of each Sew Powerful purse, and what the Sew Powerful journey meant to each of them.

I became the very proud Australian Ambassador for the Sew Powerful Purse Project. (What an honor!) The bags sewn by Aussies began arriving in my letterbox to be packaged up and sent in bulk to the U.S.

There were beautiful fabrics, impeccable sewing, and notes of empowerment inside each bag. I could not have been prouder of each contribution made by #teamaussie. I shouted it from the rooftops, writing articles in sewing magazines and blogging about this journey. I wanted everyone to know what an amazing project this was.

To top it all off, watching the live stream of the bags being unpacked was just amazing to be a part of! Just think, people from all around the globe took the time and energy to create a Sew Powerful purse for someone they had never met, knowing this will make a significant difference. What a team effort!

Australian education is top notch, it is accessible, children learn to read and write, and so much more; we are really from the lucky country. Education is powerful in creating our future.

To know that a Sew Powerful purse that I have sewn right here in Australia may help a young lady in Zambia have better access to education and therefore a brighter future means more than I can explain in words. I cannot wait to create more purses for this wonderful project. Knowing I can make a difference doing something that I love is simply fabulous.

A Piece of My Heart

By Rita Alexander
Garland Texas

I want to help others. We all feel that…we all intend to *do* that. Yet, for many of us, we are so embroiled in the day-to-day process of just living that we put off our philanthropic endeavors for a more *convenient* time.

Sadly, I am guilty of procrastinating and letting tomorrow become years later without realizing it. Another way to miss out on the opportunity to give of our talents and abilities is thinking that we can't do enough to really make a difference. *"If I can't do it in a big way, then it won't really be all that helpful."*

Sew Powerful gives everyone with any sewing ability the opportunity to make an impact. Whether your budget allows for making many purses or just one, that one will impact *one* young girl's life in such a positive way.

Although I could not participate in a *big* way, I was able to send two purses. While making these two purses, I was filled with joy, picturing the faces of the two young girls who will carry the purses that I took the time to make. I felt a *bond* with two persons whom I shall never meet, but that bond and the process of making the purses gave *me* a gift at a time when I desperately needed to feel connected to something and someone again.

Even though I have been unable to work and am currently living on a tiny fixed income, I felt that I *mattered* again, that I can still make a difference!

Certainly this extraordinary program is all about bettering the circumstances of a community in a far-off place that I will never see, but it has made a profound difference in my life as well.

Who knew when I began sewing at nine years of age that someday I would employ this skill in such a meaningful way? I will continue to be involved in whatever way that I am able, and commend and bless the persons who were led to bring such monumental change to those so in need and deserving of loving support.

I included this poem with the purses that I made:

Hello, Little One, far across the sea!
This little purse is stitched with love, a gift to you from me.

Oh, we shall never meet in person, it's true.
But now there's a piece of my heart that
you will carry with you.

It looks like a little purse, this little piece of heart
that I stitched with you in mind.
Of course, a heart can come in many shapes and kind.

Fill this little piece of heart with wondrous
things and special dreams.
Fill it with happiness till it's bursting at the seams!

Enjoy your purse, my little one, and know that every day
Someone will think of you from far, far away.

My Visit to Ngombe

By Karen Loke
Lancaster, Pennsylvania

I was fortunate to be the lucky winner of the trip to Zambia in 2015. I made several purses and sent them in, not even concerned with winning the trip—after all, how likely would that be?

Much to my surprise and delight, I received an email from Jason Miles asking me if I was "ready for Africa." I was stunned, delighted, excited, and nervous all at the same time. Wow! Imagine that, making a few little purses got me a ticket to Africa!

I started sewing over 50 years ago as a child. I continued to sew throughout my life until my children were in junior high school when homemade clothing was no longer "cool."

After a long break, I was introduced to 18" size dolls by my daughter's flower girls at her wedding. I decided to make matching dresses for their dolls and discovered Liberty Jane doll patterns. It reignited my passion for sewing and led me to Jason and Cinnamon Miles' charity, Sew Powerful.

I connected immediately with the project, the cause, the contest; everything about it just felt right to me. I have two daughters, I work at a school, and I love to sew. It all came together.

The trip to Africa was a leap of faith on my part—traveling to a foreign country with a group of strangers—and on the part of Sew

Powerful as well; they didn't know much about me, either. There was a lot of trust happening! I never doubted the people or the plan. The online presence of Liberty Jane and Sew Powerful helped me to feel that I knew Jason and Cinnamon (or at least would recognize them!).

After a very long night (eight hours sleeping on a chair at the NY airport), I finally met the group, and we were embarking on our journey to deliver the purses. What a fabulous group: Jason and Cinnamon, Barbara and Jerry, and my roommate Melinda. We trouped along through two more airports, and 15 hours later landed in Lusaka.

We were met by Esther, the most amazing woman I have ever met. You've seen her picture and read her email updates. She can move mountains! She started the Needs Care school, established a clinic, started the sewing cooperative, and is full of life and love. I truly believe there is nothing she cannot do or compel others to do. She greeted us with open arms and a big welcoming smile.

We worked very hard on that trip, and I learned a lot about myself and the ladies we met. The first obstacle was convincing them to sew the items that would become the MHM contents of the purses. It was a tall task because they had to learn how to cut, assemble and sew something they'd never seen before. After showing them the purses and explaining their part, they were given the opportunity to opt out and not participate, or jump in and make the commitment. I thought for sure there would be disagreement and discord. Esther spoke to them in their native tongue, so I'm not quite sure what she said; but the fierce look of determination on their faces was clear: they were not about to walk out and they would work as hard and fast as they could to meet the quota by the deadline. They clearly saw the value of what we were doing.

Then the project began in full swing—yards of fabric, Cinnamon at the machine demonstrating, Jason working his marketing and strategy magic, Melinda working the treadle machine.

Christopher (the only male in the program) was the official fabric cutter and machine repairman; program staff members Ruthie and Lentia supervising; Jerry, Barbara and I counting and assembling—it was coming together nicely. We were making progress, but there was a lot more to do.

We learned that soap was in short supply, and so was a change of undergarments for the girls. So, with Esther's help and local contacts, we purchased those items and they became part of the purse package. The brilliant design of the purse made it a nice presentation piece.

We also discovered that the purse would be in such demand that the girls' caretakers and extended family would each want one. So we designed a clutch style purse to contain the same items that could be given to the adult females in the household. The best part was that the sewing cooperative already had a bolt of fabric in their storage closet that was very suitable, so it could be made at no additional cost. They could sell these purses to support the project and continue to offer the donated purses for free to school girls. It was another example of rewarding collaboration.

Jason presented the ladies with the plan for gifting the girls with a purse in conjunction with their health lesson at school. He also asked them to come up with a pricing plan for selling the African-made purses; they were asked to consider the fair market value, the price point, how to market, etc. I really thought he'd lost his mind! How would these ladies know about such things? Much to my amazement, they launched into a discussion and clearly understood every bit of what Jason presented. They came up with a workable plan and were now officially businesswomen!

I learned about purposeful giving versus random donations. My instinct was to run to the closest store and buy up what they needed in sewing supplies, notions, fabric, etc., thinking they could sew faster and better with these tools. Not so. What would happen when they ran out or were broken? They could not replace them and that would leave them frustrated and back to square one.

It would be better to work with them and teach them the best way to work with what they have and can easily acquire. They didn't need random "stuff."

It became clear that the charity model for Sew Powerful is different than the usual sew-and-sell model used in many impoverished countries. These ladies are not making things to export, relying on US sales. They are making and selling something in their own community that will improve their lives and better the community. How cool is that?

When it came time to distribute the purses to the girls, it was very exciting. We presented to the class and demonstrated how the MHM products worked. We could all relate to their stories of embarrassment when they started their period in school and had no adequate protection. Especially "when you sit next to a boy and it happens," said one student. Oh, how I remember that!

When we showed them the protective layer and how the products prevented leaks, they were thrilled! They also confirmed the need for something to share with the other females in the household. Esther asked them how many pairs of underpants they each owned, and the majority of them raised their hands indicating only one or two. Can you imagine? So they were equally thrilled to be getting a few more. The purses were the icing on the cake.

The girls politely accepted their purses and thanked us. They were containing their excitement and were still on their best school behavior. But when class dismissed—chaos! They were laughing, dancing, swapping purses, and having a great time. They were typical teenagers and it was delightful to watch. We participated in a dancing party in the courtyard of the school. (I'm sure they were laughing at us most of the time.)

One young lady asked if I could find her a purse with an outer pocket, since hers did not have one. I knew we had some more assembled in the workroom, so I asked what her favorite color was. She replied by asking me what my favorite color was. When I said blue or green, she said, *"Orange, right?"* So off I went to find my new favorite color, orange! In truth, I hate orange. Absolutely abhor it! Well, for the duration of that trip, orange was indeed my favorite color (and I made a mental note to make more orange purses when I got home).

My Visit to Ngombe

The young man who drove one of the vehicles that transported us, Calvin, shared some of his story with us. He talked about walking several hours to school each day, attending class, then walking several hours home—every single day—for years! He was shocked to learn about the students at my school who complained because they didn't get the best parking spot, didn't pay attention to the teacher, or skipped class and ditched school. He simply couldn't imagine wasting the precious gift of an education. And I thought of the girls at the Needs Care school who could now go to school and not miss out on that opportunity just because they were females and it was "that time of the month."

Soon enough our African adventure came to an end. It was time to say a tearful goodbye to our host, the sewing ladies and Lusaka. They sent us off with a very moving gratitude ceremony. They thanked us for just knowing that they exist, giving something purposeful to them and their community and a chance to better their lives. We thanked them for being so inspiring and showing us what the meaning of a strong work ethic is. We prayed with them, laughed with them, and hugged them tight.

After spending time with Jason and Cinnamon, it became clear that they were very dedicated and committed to the project. They are lifelong charitable givers, mission workers, and life changers. They have made Sew Powerful a high priority in their lives and their business. It is what drives them. They are also inspiring individually and as a couple. They talk the talk and walk the walk. I trust them implicitly to do good works with the purse project and the new 3 Esthers Farm.

As a side benefit, I found out what a true support system I have in my own life: family, friends, co-workers, my employer—they all rallied around me to ensure that I could take this trip. They were all equally on board and inspired. I found out I was braver than I thought.

I traveled halfway around the world with people I never met, ate some traditional African food, slept in an airport, held a child with HIV in an impoverished slum area—things I never thought I would or could do.

My take-away from the project and the trip was this: my small gift of time (sewing some purses) gave a huge gift of time to several girls—time for an education they are so hungry for and time for a better and brighter future. Along with that, we are giving them the gift of knowing that they matter to the rest of the world.

Most importantly, the ladies of the sewing cooperative and the children and staff at the Needs Care School were the gift given to me.

I Read Every Single Word

By Theresa Dellaport

Golden, Colorado

I belong to a soap-making online forum. A member on that forum posted the Sew Powerful story and expressed her admiration of the program on July 2, 2015. I was so moved by the story, that I read every single word on their website, and looked at the pictures of the girls from Zambia over and over again.

I am an avid sewer and I am always looking for projects. I am also involved in quite a bit of charity work and found the purse project a wonderful fit for my hobby. I downloaded the purse pattern and made my first purse in about half of a day. It took me awhile to understand the directions; and I was very impressed at the simplicity, yet elegance, of the pattern.

I used up several of pieces of my fabric stash, and I was soon scouring the local fabric stores for remnants. I found many really wonderful fabrics and was very excited to match colorful and interesting fabrics together for the purse and the lining. Soon I was making several purses on the weekends.

I ended up making 24 purses, and shipped them off to Washington before the fall deadline, hoping my small contribution would make a difference in some young girl's life. I am still making purses and will continue to do so as long as there is a need.

How Could I Not Help?

By Peggy Carlson

I grew up in a family of nine. My mother died in childbirth, but our baby brother lived. We stayed together, taking care of Timmy until my father died of heart failure at age of 42. That was three years after my mom died. We were poor. I remember putting cardboard in the inside of my good shoes because they had holes in the bottoms.

Our mother was a candy maker, which supplied us with food and Christmas gifts every year. We did not know we were poor. Mom taught us all to be responsible and share the work and do a good job. I make doll clothes for the Salvation Army almost every year with a doll (which has to be 18 inches) with a wardrobe, because in spite of being poor, I was never without what I really needed.

Upon reading about those little girls needing purses for their unmentionables so that they could go to school, it really struck a chord in my heart, which I could help by making purses to send.

Knowing that Liberty Jane, along with World Vision, was willing to send sewing machines and even go there despite the perils to their lives; knowing that mothers could learn skills and support their families by sewing; how could I not help?

The truth is that many of my family members suffered at the hands of relatives, and it was kept secret. I know some of these girls probably have been bruised and battered themselves. I also know that only Jesus can show us how to forgive, how to move forward. That spirit within me says to do this. I have told my four sisters about Sew Powerful, and only one so far is helping; but in my heart I know they will help in time.

I can't go on a mission field, but I can be part of the missionary help from home. That is what God has chosen for me. Thank you for this blessing, and I will continue to sew for Sew Powerful and spread the word!

The Turning Point

By Rhondda Fanning
Australia

*M*y love of sewing started when I was a child. One of my early memories is learning to use my mother's treadle machine. My sister recently reminded me that I put the needle through my finger when I was five.

When I retired from teaching Home Economics, I discovered Liberty Jane doll clothes and the 18-inch doll world. I had three granddaughters, so I had the perfect excuse to buy dolls and sew clothes for them. I even enrolled in a Millinery course at TAFE to brush up the skills I had learned many years ago.

I had wonderful plans for all sorts of outfits and accessories. But instead, I complained about various aches and pains associated with old age that limited my ability to sit at my sewing for as long as I would like.

I was impressed with the wonderful work that Cinnamon and Jason were doing in Zambia. I really wanted to be involved. I considered asking at my church if anyone was interested in forming a group to sew the cross body purse. I had downloaded the pattern, but had not yet made one. I thought I should at least try the pattern before asking for help.

Towards the end of 2014, I noticed I was really inaccurate with my sewing at TAFE. Because we had so many assignments due, and because I was also looking after grandchildren, this was all the sewing I had time for. I blamed my problems on the fact that the class was at night, and kept hand sewing as homework to do during the day.

I decided that I definitely needed new glasses. In February 2015, I finally made an appointment with the optometrist who referred me immediately to an ophthalmologist. To my horror, I had an eye disease called Pseudo Exfoliating Syndrome. I also had a membrane growing over the macula of my left eye. I had to have immediate lens replacement in both eyes, followed by a third operation to remove the membrane covering the macula of my left eye.

By August, 2015, my ophthalmologist was pleased with my progress, but said I would have to be patient for my left eye to recover. I tried sewing, but was disappointed with the quality of my work. My ophthalmologist assured me that I could drive, but I had lost confidence. I felt as though I was losing my independence—something we all fear as we age. After not being able to drive, having poor eyesight for close work, and having to be careful after surgery, I found I spent a lot of my time browsing the Internet on my iPad—not really a very satisfying pastime.

Cinnamon's emails are always fun. I read with interest that Kylie had set up a Facebook group for people wanting to sew bags. I joined the group on a Tuesday morning. Kylie was sending completed bags to the US the following Tuesday. I had grandchildren to look after, but thought, surely I could find fabric and get at least one bag made; but could I sew? I hadn't had much success with my recent attempts.

I knew I had additional fabric somewhere, but I had to make do with what I had on hand. I still wasn't confident driving. I worried about lifting heavy boxes to look for fabric. But I did find something—not my first choice, but at least I could cut it out immediately. I really had to post my bag by Thursday when I didn't have to look after grandchildren, and was determined to make this bag.

On Thursday, I overcame my reluctance to drive and took my bag to my local post office. This was the turning point in my recovery. I've started to sew again and my close vision is finally improving. I even feel confident driving.

I don't think I would have made this progress without Cinnamon's email and Kylie's Facebook group. Thank you for your inspiration.

Moved to Tears

By Julie Sorget
Midland, Michigan

My involvement with Sew Powerful purses began when I read the book, *Unfinished-Believing Is Only The Beginning*, by Richard Stearns, President of World Vision.

The book touched my heart by challenging me, as a follower of Christ, to find my purpose and serve the Lord by giving my time, talent or treasure, to the poor and hurting in the world. Feeling unsettled and upset, I cried out to the Lord, *"What is it you want me to do?"*

The still, small voice in my head reminded me (rather loudly) of my sewing skill! I was so excited! Booting up my computer, I Googled charitable sewing, and Sew Powerful popped up. I read their mission, and was moved to tears. The peace that I felt was amazing! You see, I have some health issues, and am early retired. My unsettled feeling reading the book came from wondering how in the world I could serve in my home.

God had a plan for me, and I am so thankful that I can serve, doing it with the talent He has given me. As I sew each purse, I pray for the girl that will be receiving it.

"Truly I tell you, whatever you did for one of the least of these brothers and sisters of mine, you did for me."

Matthew 25:40

Sharing in Aqua Aerobics

By Louise Ambrosi
Leicestershire, United Kingdom

*I*first heard about the Sew Powerful project back in July 2015 via bag pattern designer Two Pretty Poppets on Facebook.

When I retired from teaching Home Economics, I discovered Liberty Jane doll clothes and the 18-inch doll world. I had three granddaughters, so I had the perfect excuse to buy dolls and sew clothes for them. I even enrolled in a Millinery course at TAFE to brush up the skills I had learned many years ago.

I was amazed and moved at how a simple thing like a bag could make such a difference in helping the young girls in Zambia stay in school. With my 10-year-old daughter Sofia (who is growing up so quickly), combined with an overflowing fabric stash and the ability to sew bags, I knew I just had to get on board.

I run my own bag-making business from my home in Loughborough, Leicestershire, UK. I have quite a large following on Facebook, Instagram, and other social media. So I immediately starting spreading the word about the project to my fellow sewers and bag-making groups, and wrote a piece on my blog inviting British folk to send their bags to me to post in one big parcel.

My promotion worked with many people joining Kylie's new Facebook group for the project, and I received several bags from fellow bag makers to add to our growing parcel. One of my fabric suppliers spotted my post and was so moved that she donated a big batch of fabric towards the cause.

I recall telling my aqua aerobics friends Alison and Donna about the project one evening, while we were jumping up and down in the water to very loud music! I knew that they could sew and they were keen to take part and learn a new bag pattern too. A mother and daughter team also, they contributed an amazing 12 bags to our big parcel from the UK, and even made their own Sew Powerful purses afterwards!

We now meet up for regularly sewing sessions and a giggle—it's so much more fun sewing together than solo! I've also gained the best friendships as a result of this project—Sew Powerful brings people together!

Sofia and I made four bags together. It was her first time reading a pattern, and she was so excited to be making bags just like mum! She helped me cut them out, and then I set up a little production line where Sofia would sew all the straight lines and I would sew the curvy or more complex sections. It was really special spending time with her, knowing that we were contributing to such an amazing cause in our small way.

In the end we collected 20 bags from the UK to send to the project by the deadline—I'm certain there were others from the UK as well—and we will continue to contribute more bags in future.

I Said, "That's For Me"

By Vivian Sylvester
Wexford, Pennsylvania

I don't think I have a story that is "book worthy," but I just wanted to tell you that I am organizing a purse sewing mission project right now. My church recently moved our fair trade store to a small strip mall in our community. Our hope is that by moving the store outside of the walls of the church, we can create opportunities for many people in our local community to become involved in "doing good things.

I believe that we all have the want and the need to make a difference. In fact, there is a sign on the store's front door which says, "Welcome! Come in and help make a difference."

I first learned about the purse project as I was scouting information on sewing for my granddaughter's American Girl doll. As a former teacher, of course, I am all for everyone having the opportunity to receive an education.

As a person who is inclined toward mission and outreach, I am all for empowering women around the world. I also was very touched when I read about each girl receiving two purses, so that if someone at home wanted one, the young girls would still have a purse for themselves so that they could attend school. When I read about such a caring and considerate ministry, I said, "That's for me!"

My enthusiasm, as I talk about the purses, has become contagious, and we have several people ready and wanting to get sewing...I can't wait!

Soon, we hope to be able to send a photo of a big stack of purses ready to ship off to young schoolgirls, and we'll be saying a prayer that they will love them.

Thank you so very much for giving girls a chance to better their lives and for giving us a wonderful project that will help our store and community make a difference.

A Win-Win-Win

By Marcy Mahle
Centerville, Ohio

*I*n the Spring of 2014, I discovered the wonderful website of Liberty Jane's Pixie Faire. To my delight, Pixie Faire had many clothing patterns for dolls from many talented designers. Eagerly, I signed up for their emails.

One day I received an email about a project called Sew Powerful, sponsored by Liberty Jane's owners Jason and Cinnamon. They supplied a purse pattern and asked their readers to make purses that would be taken to Zambia, Africa. These purses, filled with personal hygiene supplies, would be given to school-age adolescent girls.

To me, it sounded extraordinary that the girls had been missing up to six weeks of school each year. The hope was that the girls would stay in school because of these purses filled with personal hygiene supplies that helped them during menstruation. I also learned that their school was in one of the poorest sections of Lusaka, Zambia.

I was also amazed to learn that Jason and Cinnamon were sponsoring a sewing school where women learned how to sew. Both sewing and knitting machines were supplied by Sew Powerful. These women also made school uniforms for the children. The parents, who are very poor, were able to buy the uniforms at a reduced price. Also the sewers made a variety of other items that they sold. It was a win-win-win for everyone involved and the best part was that everyone kept his or her self-respect. They were not simply given money. The sewers were taught a means to earn a living, the parents bought the uniforms, and the girls stayed in school, securing the hope of a future.

Once again in 2015, I received another message about the second year of Sew Powerful purses. I printed out the pattern and got to work. This year, I decided to spread the word amongst my family and friends. Thankfully many of them are now including Sew Powerful amongst the organizations they give donations to.

Sew Powerful is a wonderful organization that gives people the tools to help themselves and to keep their self-respect. I pray that it will keep growing and that its help will spread to many more in need. May God bless Jason and Cinnamon in all their good work.

Long-Term Impact

By Maryann Gubala
Wilbraham, Massachusetts

I am a college student, and therefore, I am quite busy and don't have a lot of money. Still, I'm always looking for ways to help and serve others. I believe that as a Christian, that is what I am called to do.

While I sometimes complain about classes or the workload, I am incredibly blessed to be able to attend college. I know that many people around the world, especially girls, cannot even finish high school or the equivalent. The thought that some girls stop attending school because of something natural (periods) is just crazy to me. When I heard about Sew Powerful, I knew it was a cause that I wanted to support if possible.

I remember when I was in middle school and hit puberty. I was so embarrassed by my period, even though it was completely normal and natural. I was terrified of leaking through my pants and the embarrassment that would result. I simply cannot fully imagine being in those circumstances without the disposable products specifically engineered for menstruation that we have here in the United States today.

The facts that some girls have to use rags or whatever else they can find and that many girls stop attending school because of their periods breaks my heart. Periods are annoying and painful enough without the embarrassment of leaking. I know that I would not feel comfortable going to school at all if I had to miss school for one week every month. I do not want anyone to know when that time of the month hits, even though it is a natural phenomenon.

This project reminded me how incredibly fortunate I am that I can continue life as normal when my period hits. My heart breaks over the fact that not all girls are as fortunate. This project has helped me realize how much periods can be detrimental to a girl's schooling and therefore future. Every time my period comes, I have a newfound appreciation for access to products designed for menstruation and the ability to still go on with my day-to-day life.

As I mentioned before, I am in college. Therefore, I have limited free time and limited funds. Still, God has made a way for me to sew for Sew Powerful.

For several years now, I have been sewing for Dress a Girl Around the World. I started working with that project because it seemed like a good way to help impoverished girls, even with my time and financial constraints. I sew when I have time or just need a break from school. I do not have to be anywhere at a specific time.

Over the past few years, people have donated money and materials to the cause and that helps me continue sewing, even when my personal funds are extremely low. I never expected to still be sewing dresses several years later, but apparently God had other plans. Since I'm still sewing dresses, I have lots of scrap materials. Many of these scraps are too small for other dresses, but big enough to become parts of the Sew Powerful bags.

I also sew some things for craft fairs, and have lots of heavier weight scraps from those projects. When I heard about the Sew Powerful project, I loved the cause and realized that I had materials already available for several purses.

The pattern was a little more challenging than I was accustomed to, but I figured it was worth a try. I found that making purses was somewhat addicting; before I knew it, I had sixteen of them for the shipment in October. I had originally planned to make only half a dozen. I have also made one for myself, which sometimes serves as a conversation starter about Sew Powerful.

In addition to being a great cause (helping girls stay in school after puberty), I love how the Sew Powerful project operates. I love how women in Zambia are being trained to sew and make the hygiene kits. I believe this creates the opportunity for real lasting impact that is not possible with just handouts of pre-made hygiene kits.

The project seems like it was planned for long-term impact rather than short-term. I love programs that seek to help and serve impoverished people in strategic ways, and Sew Powerful seems to do just that. I look forward to sewing more purses as time allows. I'm thankful to be a part of this amazing initiative.

Cinnamon Was A Student Of Mine

By Tenney Singer
Montesano, Washington

I found out about Sew Powerful because Cinnamon Miles was a student of mine many years ago. I was interested in seeing what her life had become. I was amazed at what she had accomplished in the years since I had last seen her.

The purse project grabbed me: I like to sew, I have a lot of material "leftovers" on hand, and I like to help people in need. This project seemed like a perfect way to use the skills and resources at hand to bless girls in Africa.

I made one purse and felt pleased at the result. So I thought I'd do a couple more and send off three of them. I did that. But then I looked at the piles of cloth still in my storage bin, and decided I'd make an even ten for the project. I had so much fun designing and decorating them, and the last seven were quickly made and sent off.

I will definitely get involved in this project again, and I have friends that also want to do it. We will have a purse party and see how many we can get done together.

God Used My Mistake

By Candace Carroll

Texas

I first heard about the Sew Powerful ministry when I was attending a business conference with my family. Though it was a business conference, that year there was a special emphasis on using our money, influence and businesses to help others in need rather than through charitable giving, our time or some other way.

Jason Miles was there to speak about his area of expertise in business, but also to present what he and his wife, Cinnamon, had done to help others in need. I was very intrigued by the Sew Powerful project; but when Jason began to give statistics about how badly the girls needed feminine hygiene products—I was stunned.

I immediately got on my phone right during his talk and began to look at the statistics myself. I was utterly shocked with what I found! I had no idea that in many countries, feminine hygiene products are considered a luxury and are often taxed! In third world countries, you would be lucky to find anything at all. My heart went out to those girls who were missing school because they had nothing at all.

When I got back home, my mom and I began to go through our leftover fabric to see what we could use to start making purses. I had a lot of different leftover fabrics from different projects, but one large piece of beige denim caught my eye. And that is when I realized in amazement that God had been providing for those girls even before I knew about Sew Powerful.

A few years ago, I had wanted to make a nice, beige denim skirt for myself. Still somewhat learning how to sew, I had bought way too much fabric for what I needed! I could have literally made two skirts with all that I bought!

After making the skirt, I stowed the several yards I had left away, figuring that I would use it sometime for something. When I came across it again with the other leftover fabrics I had, I remembered what had happened. God used my seeming mistake of buying way too much fabric to bless those girls in Africa.

So far, I have been able to make seven purses out of that fabric I have, and will probably be able to make many more. I consider it a great privilege to take part in Sew Powerful and to come alongside the ladies in Africa and help them where I can.

We Built a Community

By Mary Reese
Alverno College, Milwaukee, Wisconsin

When I first learned about the *Sew Powerful* project, I knew that I had to get involved. I work for Alverno College, a women's college in Milwaukee, Wisconsin, that emphasizes service to the community.

For almost 130 years, we have been dedicated to the education of women, inspiring them to reach their fullest potential. I thought, "What a perfect fit!" I organized a group of seamstresses from across campus—students, faculty and staff—to begin sewing purses.

We were not only giving of our time and talents, we were helping to empower young women halfway around the world, allowing them to stay in school, and in turn, investing in their success. And isn't that what it's all about? A sisterhood, reaching across miles, borders, even oceans, to lift each other up and support one another so that we may all benefit from each individual's triumphs.

I'm proud to say that together we sewed 20 purses. Some of us have been sewing a long time; some of us are truly beginners. But together, we built a community of women working for a single cause, one stitch at a time.

I Couldn't Believe My Eyes

By Pam VanOteghem

Leesburg, Georgia

My journey with the Sew Powerful Purse Project began with an unexpected gift of a Bernina embroidery machine.

My neighbors were clearing out and having a yard sale. They brought over a large tub and asked me if I wanted it, knowing that I love to sew. "We just want the empty tub back."

I couldn't believe my eyes! We emptied the tub and made a quick inventory of what was missing, broken or mysterious (never having owned an embroidery machine, it was all mysterious), and set out to the nearest Bernina dealer with the machine for inspection and service.

During the two-hour drive to the Bernina dealer, we set a budget for parts replacement and supplies, not knowing that I was entering a completely new world of sewing. It was while the machine was in for service that the idea of the purses kept coming up.

I decided that the machine should be used to help give back and every purse I've sent has been embroidered. No two are alike, and all are made with love and prayer. I hope every purse carries a little of the generosity and good will that made them possible. I have even transferred the pattern to Plexiglas to make fussy cutting and design easier.

If my little embroidered purses can keep a girl in school, my efforts to learn the complexities of machine embroidery have been rewarded. Thank you, Sew Powerful!

God Just Keeps Blessing Us

By Marilyn McMullen

The group of ladies that I belong to and lead is called Lydia's Helping Hands. Our scripture reference is Proverbs 31:13. We are self-supporting and we receive a lot of donations for our sewing needs.

We meet once a week on Thursdays, but some of us do a lot more sewing at home, as we seem to get more done at home. We make things for the nursing homes, shut-ins, hospice and VA Hospitals.

Some of the things we make are adult bibs, walker bags, lap throws, catheter bags, and cancer hats. We get phone calls from time to time asking for special requests of things a patient might need.

Our church is very supportive of what we are doing. We have craft shows occasionally to earn money to buy supplies that we might need. We also give to missions.

Our group of ladies is very small and most of us are retired. We enjoy getting together for the fellowship and for sharing ideas. We have a day where we can get together and laugh, cry, and share with each other. God just keeps blessing us over and over with so many supplies.

One of the ladies heard about the Sew Powerful Purse program and shared it with us, so we decided to make some for the girls in Africa. We are a little slow at getting things done, but we really enjoy what we do. Some of us have health problems, and our fingers don't work as quickly as they used to; but we do the best we can.

When we make the cross body bags, it puts a smile in our hearts to think of some young lady or girl that will be getting it. To think of her smile is all the reward we need. We give God all the glory for what we do, and we thank you for the opportunity to do this. God Bless.

Practical Pieces

By Linda McGowan

Wilton, Maine

From the earliest remembrances of my life, I have had a love for needle and thread and the possibilities these tools allow me to accomplish. Those first stitches were large and the projects small. As I matured in age and ability, my stitches became smaller, and the projects larger.

By the time I was 12, my mother encouraged my talents and allowed me to use her Singer sewing machine. It was love at first stitch!

When I bought my first sewing machine, the salesclerk told me, *No other machine in your home will pay for itself over and over if you use it well.* He spoke truth.

For 60 years, I have sewn clothing, home decor of all sorts, sports equipment, wardrobe accessories, quilts—you name it, I've tried it!

The LORD has given me ability and allowed me to purchase tools to pursue my love of sewing. I have been blessed to share all with young girls and older women, teaching them to express themselves in thread and fabric.

Practical pieces have always been my project preference; so when my adult daughter introduced me to this Sew Powerful purse program, I couldn't wait to get started. We shopped for fabric thinking of the young African girls who would use the purses. The process of completing the purses was a joy, given a good pattern and clear directions.

As a woman, mother of two girls, grandmother to five girls, and mentor to many young girls in homemaking skills, this cross body purse project and the reason behind the purse program struck a chord in my heart. It was with great joy that I completed a dozen purses and now support the program financially.

For those in the Zambian sewing cooperative, I pray they may know the same sense of fulfillment for their efforts at their machines as I have for nearly 70 years.

Blessings to Sew Powerful for this opportunity and the blessing it has brought to my life—touching lives outside of my state and country.

Please Forgive Me

By Toby Capps

P lease forgive me! Those are the words I will never forget. I heard them as I met an amazing woman in South Africa on my first trip to that beautiful country.

Let me take you back several years before Jason and Cinnamon created Sew Powerful. Jason helped create a program called Caregiver Kits. The program allowed my corporation, McKesson, to partner with World Vision and churches, corporations, and community groups from all over the United States. Together we provided medical supplies to remote villages to assist in their fight against the AIDS pandemic. We later learned that Esther has 90 of these caregivers helping at Needs Care School.

In South Africa we visited a group of seamstresses working hard with very limited and antiquated equipment. They were sewing blankets their small village needed. We were amazed at their passion and work ethic. They weren't sewing to earn money for themselves, but instead were using the profits to raise an orphan and buy medical supplies to help people in their village!

Then we visited one of the caregivers - Mrs. Sgelum. She was a beneficiary of the hard work of the seamstresses. We took a small trail to the very top of a hill overlooking the village. There was a small hut with just a few possessions inside. But to our surprise Mrs. Sgelum was nowhere to be found.

Suddenly we saw her running up the trail towards the home. Finally reaching the top she said, *"Please forgive me, I was helping to bury one of my neighbors."*

No other explanation—almost without emotion. As the tears welled up in my eyes, she went on to introduce us to her grandchildren.

This speaks volumes about the lives and work ethic of every one of the caregivers and seamstresses we have had to opportunity to meet. Mrs. Sgelum changed my life! God bless you Mrs. Sgelum.

Thank you for your tremendous support of Sew Powerful and the people they work so hard to support!

PART FIVE

7 Days in Ngombe

"The real voyage of discovery consists not in seeking new landscapes, but in having new eyes."

—Marcel Proust

Section Introduction

By Jason

We realize that 99.9% of our partners will never have the opportunity to visit Ngombe, see the children, or sit down and get to know the seamstresses. But if you did go with us to Zambia on one of our annual trips, then each morning we'd sit at breakfast and do a simple devotional together. We'd talk about what we saw the day before and prepare ourselves for the day ahead.

The trip devotional we use was written by Dr. Andy Smith. He's a Pastor, Theologian, and Sew Powerful board member. He also visited the Needs Care School in 2009.

Since you probably won't be able to go with us, we thought we'd do the next best thing and organize your virtual Seven-Day Vision Trip. Ready to go?

In this chapter, I'll share the daily trip schedule and then the devotional Andy wrote for that day. We'd encourage you to actually do the devotional with us over a seven-day period. Take a week to immerse yourself in the trip to Ngombe.

Companion Photos and Videos

To make your trip come alive, we've prepared a day-by-day photo and video presentation. We'd encourage you to watch it as you go through this chapter. That way you can see the sites, the beautiful children, and the amazing seamstresses.

See it at

www.sewpowerful.org/7-days-in-ngombe/

Use This as a Group Bible Study

If you have a Bible study group you lead or participate in, then consider using this material creatively. For example, turn this into a seven-week study by taking on one day each time you meet over seven weeks. Buy a copy of this book for each member of your group, and consider it your virtual group trip. If you'd like a stand-alone copy of the devotional guide you can get a copy at the same location:

www.sewpowerful.org/7-days-in-ngombe/

More About Andy Smith: Andy is a board member at Sew Powerful and is the Executive Pastor at Saint Matthews Lutheran Church in Walnut Creek, California. He has served in ministry for thirty years and holds a Doctorate from Princeton Theological Seminary.

Let's begin...

Monday
Day One In Ngombe

oday we'll be leaving the hotel at 9:00 am and driving for twenty minutes to Ngombe Compound. You'll be amazed at how much like home the hotel already feels, even after just one night. The room was nice; the breakfast was great, and the staff very friendly.

The long trip to Zambia the day before was exhausting, but you're energized by the opportunity to finally see the Sew Powerful program. Anticipation is high as Esther arrives, greets us, and then says, *"Okay, let's go."*

Entering Ngombe: As we enter Ngombe, you'll notice the difficulty of driving on the dirt roads filled with giant potholes, the crowded streets with people walking in every direction, and all the children barefoot, unattended, and playing in the streets.

Welcoming Ceremony: As we arrive, you'll be surprised to see hundreds of children sitting in the courtyard, eagerly waiting for our arrival. We park quickly and walk over to a row of seats that have been set up for us—directly in front of the children. We are the guests of honor. The program begins with the children singing. Each class does a song or two. During the program, we are asked to introduce ourselves, greet the children; and if we are unlucky, we even have to sing a song.

The ceremony lasts for several hours; and then as the assembly breaks up, we are shown the Principal's Office, which is our new home away from home at Needs Care. We can leave our belongings, come back to get a drink, and take a break when needed.

Serving Lunch: After we get settled, we are asked to begin helping set up lunch. We tour the kitchen and notice they don't have any appliances. They cook the meal of porridge in giant pots over a wood fire. We carry the pots out into the courtyard and the children line up to receive a scoop. Small plastic containers appear, we're not sure where they were hidden before, but each child has one.

Each child takes their porridge, goes and sits down in groups, and begins eating. We notice that before they are finished, they place lids on their containers. They are going to take half of it back home for their siblings and other family members.

Meeting The Children: From the moment we arrive at Needs Care, even though there are a sea of faces, individual children begin to stand out. During lunch we ask them their names, and we quickly find we have newfound friends.

Meeting The Seamstresses: After lunch, we finally get to spend time greeting the seamstresses, seeing the sewing room, and learning about how they do their work.

Of course, we jump in to help; they don't mind having all the fabric cutting help they can get. We are on cloud nine. As the work progresses we slow down, begin asking questions, asking them to repeat their names until we remember, and start to make friends. Kindred spirits.

Our Exotic Zambian Lunch: After an hour of sewing room bliss, we are interrupted by Jason who says, *"Our lunch is ready."* We eat in Esther's office—to our surprise the meal includes Zambian specialties. Today's menu: fried chicken, vegetables and Shima, which is like very thick cream of wheat made from corn.

Afternoon Tour: The afternoon includes a full tour of the school, clinic, and nearby church where the school started. We learn about the adult literacy classes, peek in the kitchen again, see the small library, and listen as the teachers give lessons to packed rooms—more children than we can comprehend. Then it's back to the sewing room for more fun with the seamstresses.

Departure For The Hotel: Four o'clock comes way too fast, and we have to head back to the hotel. The afternoon traffic is bad, so it takes longer to get back. After getting cleaned up, we head off to dinner and then all too quickly, day one is done.

Theirs Is the Kingdom

"Blessed are the poor in spirit, for theirs is the Kingdom."
Matthew 5:3 (NIV)

I life-changing encounter between Jesus and a man suffering from the effects of a cruel disease called leprosy.

In the days of Jesus, a person with leprosy was an outcast from the society in which he or she lived. Please take time each day to reflect on this brief encounter between Jesus and a man suffering with this disease. Allow the Lord to speak to you about your personal encounter with the poor in spirit.

Read Mark 1:40-42...

"A man with leprosy came to Jesus and begged him on his knees, 'If you are willing, you can make me clean.' Filled with compassion, Jesus reached out his hand and touched the man, 'I am willing,' he said, 'Be clean!' Immediately the leprosy left him and he was cured."

Mark 1:40-42 (NIV)

When chronic problems becomes personal

The physical discomforts of leprosy were horrible, but the emotional pain and suffering were devastating. People with leprosy were the "untouchables" in society. They were forced to live outside of the community, unable to attend public worship, and had to shout a warning, "Unclean!" to anyone coming near them. They often died internally of loneliness, despair and rejection long before the disease took over their physical bodies.

One day, Jesus encountered a man with leprosy and this great humanitarian crisis became very personal to him. He saw the cruel disease in the face of a human being. All of a sudden, the disease of leprosy had a face. The writer of this story doesn't say, "A leper came to Jesus." He says a man with leprosy came to Jesus. Leprosy had invaded the life of a precious human being. When leprosy became personal for Jesus, he wept. This week you might weep as the challenges of Zambia become personal to you.

- ✓ HIV and AIDS is a disease ravaging the lives of human beings that are precious to our God. My guess is that the HIV and AIDS pandemic in Sub-Saharan Africa will become very personal for you this week as Ngombe Compound has the highest concentration of HIV and AIDS in Zambia.

- ✓ The orphan crisis caused by AIDS/TB/Malaria has a massive impact in Zambia with over one million orphaned children currently living in a country of 14–16 million people. Ngombe Compound is home to the highest concentration of these orphans in any urban community.

- ✓ Food insecurity and extreme hunger are devastating the poorest members of the Ngombe Compound, with many having no regular supply of food and living on less than one full meal a day.

- ✓ Basic personal care items such as feminine hygiene supplies are impossible for the poor. These and other basic care issues are out of sight, but if you inquire and take the time to get to know your new acquaintances, you'll discover they are very real issues.

Monday

Please pray, "O Lord, may I encounter you in new and fresh ways this week as I encounter the people of Ngombe Compound."

Tuesday

Day Two In Ngombe

*W*e meet in the lobby at 9:00 am again. Now we have the routine all figured out. We greet Esther and prepare for a fun day.

Entering Ngombe: Ngombe feels familiar now. The sights, the sounds, and the smells have all become something we don't fear or wonder about. They are part of our reality. As we arrive, children are already in their classes.

Special Projects: This morning we spend time showing the seamstresses new techniques. But we also realize the Zambian seamstresses know what they are doing. They know their machines and their process. They aren't entry-level seamstresses and they are there to work. We realize they are moving fast and focused on their activities.

Our Exotic Zambian Lunch: The morning rushes by and our sewing room bliss is once again interrupted by Jason who says, "Our lunch is ready." We enter Esther's office and wonder what we'll eat. Today's menu—oxtail in a nice meat sauce, with vegetables and Shima.

Afternoon Purse Packing: We spend the afternoon helping the seamstresses by packing hundreds of purses with the liners and shields, underwear and soap. We marvel at all the amazing purses we see and stop to chat about them every few minutes. We keep secretly looking for a purse that we have made and a celebratory cheer goes up every time we find one.

Departure For The Hotel: Today, four o'clock doesn't come as fast, and we realize that packing purses is hard work. Once again the afternoon traffic is bad, so it takes longer to get back; but we expected it, so it's not so bad. After getting cleaned up, we head off to dinner and then all too quickly, day two is done.

TUESDAY DEVOTIONAL
Theirs Is the Kingdom

"A man with leprosy came to Jesus…"

*T*he man in this story was *drawn* to Jesus. One who knew rejection and stigma was attracted to the Savior. Jesus intentionally and passionately engaged with those who were not welcome elsewhere.

The broken and marginalized people knew he liked them. Do they know we like them?

✓ Where do men and women in our community who are suffering with the effects of HIV and AIDS go to church? Are they welcome in our circles of friends?

✓ Where are the orphans in our community and are we looking after them?

✓ Are there widows in our midst that don't have the support and help they need?

Do these people feel *drawn* to be with us? Do we feel drawn to serve them?

In Psalm 8:4-5, the Psalmist declares, *"What is man that you are mindful of him, the son of man that you care for him? You made him a little lower that the heavenly beings and **crowned him with glory and honor.**"*

187

Jesus had a way of seeing and treating every person he met as if he/she were royalty. He honored them, and they felt his affirmation. This man was made in the image of God and was precious to Jesus.

Jesus viewed every person he encountered as if they were Kings and Queens wearing crowns. The broken, marginalized, and sinful men and women of his day ran to be with him. They knew he cared. They knew he loved them.

Please pray, *"O Lord, help me to see and honor every person I meet today as if he/she was wearing a crown."*

Wednesday
Visiting 3 Esthers Farm

W̶e meet in the lobby at 9:00 am again, but today is different. We need to bring a hat and some mosquito repellant because today we are headed to the 3 Esthers Farm instead of Ngombe. We greet Esther and prepare for a fun day.

Buying Fruit Trees: The farm is located about forty minutes from the hotel. On the way, we stop at a beautiful English garden nursery and stroll through the rows of plants. We each pick out three- foot tall trees: orange, guava, or mango.

As we leave, we look back and take in the view one last time. It's such a beautiful place! We didn't expect to find that in Lusaka. The trees cost just a few dollars each, but we pay in Kwacha, the local currency. We fit the small trees into the vehicles carefully and enjoy a fun ride the rest of the way to the farm.

Farm Tour: We arrive at the farm mid-morning and are greeted by Nicholas and Lillian, the farm caretakers, as well as Tiger, the cute farm dog. The farm is vibrant and well organized.

The farm tour begins, and Nicholas has us walk the entire property with him. As we walk around the edge of the ten acres, Nicholas stops and explains things as we go. As we walk, we go slowly, asking a lot of questions, and the tour takes longer than we expected.

Picnic Lunch: Today our lunch includes an apple, a granola bar, some dried fruit, and a bottle of water. Simple items that we bought the night before at a local grocery store near the hotel.

As we eat together, under the shade of a cute African style hut that Nicholas built for his guests, we discuss the farm, the potential impact on the children of Ngombe, and the lunch of porridge we had served them earlier in the week.

We begin to realize exactly what it would take to help the moms achieve their goal of providing a healthy lunch for the children of Needs Care. We think of the children we've met—our newfound friends. We imagine their lunch someday being beans, Shima, vegetables, oranges, and maybe even meat or eggs.

Afternoon Tree Planting: We spend the afternoon helping to plant the fruit trees we brought. Nicholas does most of the digging ahead of time, shows us how to plant them just right, and then we begin watering the trees. That takes longer than we expected, because we have to use a watering can and fetch water. We end the day with a prayer over the trees and the farm.

Departure For The Hotel: We start the journey back to the hotel. This time it's longer, but the change of scenery is fun. We see the sights of the Zambian countryside. We struggle through the Lusaka afternoon traffic, but soon we're back at the hotel. After getting cleaned up we head off to dinner and then all too quickly, day three is done.

When A Statistic Has A Name

*"…and begged him on his knees,
'If you are willing you can make me clean.' "*

The greatest humanitarian crisis of all time is happening on our watch. Worldwide, over 35 million people have already died as a result of complications related to HIV and AIDS, and another 36 million are currently living with the HIV virus.

- ✓ Approximately 3,000 people die every day as a result of complications from this horrible disease.

- ✓ Every day, about 5,753 people contract HIV—about 240 every hour.

- ✓ In 2015, 36.7 million people were living with HIV.

- ✓ As of December 2105, 17 million people living with HIV (46% of the total) had access to antiretroviral therapy.

And in East and Southern Africa, according to Amfarm:

- ✓ In 2015 there were 19 million people living with HIV (more than half of them women).

- ✓ It is estimated that more than 960,000 people became newly infected.

- ✓ In 2015 470,000 people died of AIDS-related causes.
- ✓ East and Southern Africa account for 46% of the global total of new HIV infections.

To see additional statistics visit:

http://amfar.org/About-HIV-and-AIDS/About-HIV/AIDS/

The statistics are numbing. They often leave us unable to do anything…until this week, when these overwhelming statistics will have names.

After approaching Jesus, this man falls to his knees. Jesus is moved. Jesus is now looking at leprosy in the face of one human being and hearing the voice of one man who is suffering. Leprosy has now become personal for Jesus. This man has a name. He has a family. He has dreams. He has a story. He is drawn to Jesus because he still has hope.

This week, we will all encounter HIV and AIDS in the faces of one or more of the children we meet at the school in Zambia. They all have names. They all have dreams.

I'd encourage you to take notes this week and remember the names and stories of the people you meet. Put yourself in their shoes. The greatest humanitarian crisis of all time will become very personal for you as you make new friends, and commit to caring for these precious people.

Please pray, *"O Lord, allow me to see and hear the story of a child in ways that will change me forever."*

Thursday

Back In Ngombe

᳀

*W*e meet in the lobby at 9:00 am again. We're excited for another chance to spend time with the seamstresses and children at Needs Care. Esther arrives and we are quickly on our way.

Entering Ngombe: Today we drive a different route to Ngombe. As we make our way through the streets, we are shocked at the grandeur of the homes. There is wealth, just minutes away from extreme poverty. Similar to Tuesday, as we arrive, children are already in their classes.

Morning Clinic Visit: This morning we start by walking across the street and visiting the school clinic. There are neighborhood patients quietly waiting on benches outside in the courtyard. We enter the small house that has been converted into a clinic and meet Loveness, the nurse. We are really impressed with her skills and ask a lot of questions. But we realize patients are waiting, so hurry back to the Needs Care School.

Purse Packing: Today we are excited because a group of girls will receive the health training and their purses. We work hard helping the seamstresses by packing up additional purses. We also carefully prepare the purses that we made at home and brought with us on the trip. We can't wait to meet the girls that will receive them.

Our Exotic Zambian Lunch: As has happened every day we've been at Needs Care, the morning rushes, Jason says it's lunch-time, and we enter Esther's office, this time with anticipation over what we might see on the menu. Today it's deep-friend whole fish, tilapia, with vegetables and Shima.

Purse Distribution: Just after lunch, we begin setting up for the afternoon health training and purse distribution. Esther guides us and we use a large classroom. We nervously arrange the purses, double check things, and ask unnecessary questions, mainly because we're nervous. What we really wonder is if the girls will like the purses, especially the one's we've personally made.

The girls quickly stream into the room and find their seats. The room is filled with energy and laughter as Esther calls the class to order. She speaks to the girls for a long time in a very engaging way. But it's in Nyanja, the local language, so we can't understand everything she's saying. We wish we knew their language. But we get the idea and on occasion we hear an English sounding word or two.

Esther asks Cinnamon to explain the use of the shields and liners. Then she asks the girls to make a promise to stay in school all month if they receive a purse and supplies. They all shout loudly, "Yes!" And the girls come up, one at a time, and receive two purses—one purse for themselves, and one for a sister, auntie, mom, or caretaker in their household.

After the health class is over, we mingle with the girls for pictures, conversations, and encouragement. More hugs than you can remember. Each one a godsend as you realize you receive more from this program than you could ever give.

Departure For The Hotel: Today, Jason has to drag you out of the classroom as you stop to say one last goodbye. Four o'clock came way too fast. On the way back we talk all about the girls we met, the stories we heard, and the joy we felt. Our hearts sink as we realize tomorrow is our last day at Needs Care. After getting cleaned up, we head off to dinner and then all too quickly, day four is done.

THURSDAY DEVOTIONAL
Poverty and the Heart of God

"Filled with compassion, Jesus…"

After seeing leprosy in the face of the man on his knees, and hearing the cry of his voice begging for mercy, Jesus is filled with compassion. "Compassion" means to "suffer with."

Jesus allows his heart to be wrenched. The God who spun the heavens now has tears welling up in his eyes. His bottom lip is beginning to quiver. The heart of Jesus is moved as he suffers with this broken human being who is kneeling at his feet.

This week is really not about…

- ✓ HIV/AIDS, TB or Malaria
- ✓ Orphans or widows
- ✓ Food insecurity or farming
- ✓ Sew Powerful purses or purse makers
- ✓ Seamstresses or adolescent girls in Africa
- ✓ You or your need to participate

This week is truly about the heart of God. People who suffer are very close to the heart of God. May they be close to our hearts as well—and may we find ways to align our personal mission and purpose in service to Him and them.

Almost 60 years ago, Bob Pierce, the founder of World Vision, allowed his heart to be broken while holding in his arms a little girl who had recently been abandoned by her family. His prayer that day has become famous, and I'd encourage you to pray it today.

Please pray, *"Let my heart to be broken by the things that break the heart of God."*

Friday
Our Last Day at Needs Care

We meet in the lobby at 9:00 am again, slightly depressed because we realize Friday has come too quickly, and it's our last day at Needs Care. Esther arrives and we are quickly on our way.

Entering Ngombe: Today, as we drive into Ngombe, we try to take in every detail; we point out things we hadn't noticed before. We are already anticipating that we'll miss this place.

Bursting at the Seams: We spend the morning helping the seamstresses. We take turns cutting, folding, and sitting next to them as they work. We feel bolder to ask them questions, and want to make sure we remember as much of their story as we can. We hear new details that shock us, inspire us, and help us fill in the blanks. We are bursting at the seams to bond with these kindred spirits.

Our Exotic Zambian Lunch: All too soon Jason says it's lunch-time. It's our last exotic lunch in Ngombe. Today's menu—beef stew over Shima.

Surprise Guests: After lunch, Esther lets us know that we are going to be spending the afternoon with young ladies who have received purses. They will come in, one at a time, and greet us and share their story. We can ask them questions about their life and understand how the program is making a difference. We are nervous for them, but can't wait to begin.

Mary: Esther walks in with Mary; introduces her and then steps out as Mary sits down. She's nervous and unsure of herself. But we smile, introduce ourselves, tell her we're glad to meet her and that she doesn't need to be nervous at all.

Mary tells us her story and begins to settle in, smile, and become more relaxed. She is in sixth grade. She lives with her auntie; her mom and dad have passed away. She has two brothers, three sisters, and lots of cousins. She thanks us for the purse, and tells us the items have really helped a lot.

We can't help ourselves. We begin asking questions, one at a time, slowly, and sitting on pins and needles with each answer. The questions are general at first, like if she has a Secondary School she plans to attend.

But then we ask about how she uses the purse and products. She shares openly and is surprisingly candid. She proudly declares she hasn't missed any days of school since she received her purse last August. We try not to cry.

As we feel the conversation winding down, our questions turn into comments. We begin to offer words of encouragement, advice, and care. We quickly become cheerleaders for Mary. She thanks us and then leaves.

Esther re-enters the room, asks us how the conversation went and we all say, "Great!" We can't wait to meet the next girl. Then Esther drops a bombshell on us. Mary is HIV Positive. We hadn't thought of that possibility until that moment. It rattles us, but we realize we don't have time to process the emotions.

Agnes quickly comes in...

Then Kristina...

Then Joy...

Then Rachel...

Friday

The young women we meet are awe-inspiring. They are brave, funny, articulate, and caring. We are surprised to learn that some have even divided their shields and liners and shared them with a friend who didn't receive a purse. Some explain their personal struggles, the loss of parents, brothers and sisters. Some share their dreams.

Departure for the Hotel: We end the day taking pictures with the seamstresses, saying goodbye, and soaking in the final moments at Needs Care. On the way back, we talk a little, but most of us are silent. We think about the girls we met, wonder about their futures, and say a little prayer for them in our minds. We're at the hotel before we realize it. After getting cleaned up, we head off to dinner. Then, all too quickly, day five is done.

FRIDAY DEVOTIONAL
A Question Of Will

"I am willing, Jesus said..."

Once Jesus sees, hears and feels the effects of leprosy in the life of the man kneeling at his feet, he is left with a question of will.

Is he willing to do something?

The ministry of Sew Powerful is providing people all over the world with the opportunity to see, hear, and feel, in a very personal way, the effects of extreme poverty on the lives of children in Africa.

Thousands of people are now involved in making purses; but only a handful have actually been able to come and see the program, meet the people, and experience the full impact of the work.

Now that you've met Esther, the seamstresses, teachers, and students, you are left with a simple set of questions:

✓ What are you willing to do?

✓ What will your family do?

✓ What will your Bible Study or Small Group do?

✓ What will your church do?

I'd encourage you to consider how you can engage your skills, abilities, social circles, and financial resources to make a bigger difference in the program. If:

✓ you're a gifted communicator, then tell the story.

✓ you're a gifted administrator, then organize events.

✓ you're blessed financially, then give generously.

An old proverb says, "A confused mind always says no." Believe it or not, many times people return from places like Ngombe, and because of the paralysis of not knowing exactly how to help, and feeling overwhelmed, they end up not doing anything at all. Please don't let that be your ultimate story.

I'd encourage you to battle being overwhelmed and confused about what your next steps should be, and simply step out in faith. Work with Jason, Cinnamon, the Sew Powerful board, and the team leaders in Ngombe to implement specific and actionable plans, and trust God in the process.

What are you willing to do in order to combat extreme poverty and make a difference in the lives of the women and children of Zambia? Whatever it is—do it.

Please pray, *"O Lord, please begin to show me how I can make a difference in offering hope to my new friends in Zambia."* close to the heart of God. *May they be close to our hearts as well—and may we find ways to align our personal mission and purpose in service to Him and them.*

Saturday

Our Planning Day

*T*oday's schedule is different. After breakfast and devotions, we meet at 10:00 am to travel an hour outside Lusaka to the Protea Lodge. It's a beautiful setting, where we get to go on an hour-long game drive and see zebras, lions, kudu and several other animals. Protea is a beautiful place, but too small to have elephants, giraffes, or any of the other large African animals. We have a nice lunch and spend the afternoon on a very important assignment.

Reflections and Personal Planning: Today has a serious purpose as well. We are challenged to journal our reflections of the time we've spent at Needs Care. Jason guides us to discuss ideas related to how we can get more involved in the mission and purpose of Sew Powerful. Questions include:

- ✓ How can we stay involved after we return home?
- ✓ Who do we know that we can tell about Sew Powerful?
- ✓ What personal goals do we want to make related to our participation?

Departure For The Hotel: We end the day taking group photos, walking around the property in quiet personal reflection, and enjoying the beauty of Africa. Back at the hotel, we get cleaned up head off to dinner; and then, all too quickly, day six is done.

Touching The Untouchables

"Jesus reached out his hand and touched the man…"

I like to believe that Jesus reached out and touched the man right on one of his "untouchable" sores. In touching the man with leprosy, Jesus was branding himself as unclean. He was breaking all the religious and social mores of his day. He was stepping outside of his comfort zone.

Why

Why did Jesus physically touch the man? Couldn't he have just proclaimed, "Be clean!"?

When Jesus spoke to the wind and the waves to "Be still!" the Sea of Galilee became as smooth as glass. Jesus had the power to change nature by simply lifting his voice, *"He lifts his voice, the earth melts"* (Ps. 46:6).

The man had probably not been touched physically by another human being in years. He was not only in need of physical healing. He desperately needed emotional healing.

The poor don't just need financial support, they need:

- ✓ Encouragement
- ✓ Friendship
- ✓ Emotional support

✓ Long-term partnership

✓ A relationship with caring people

Jesus is concerned about the whole person. Can you imagine what was going through the mind of the man as he felt the human touch and affirmation of another human being? He must have been overwhelmed.

I pray that our encounters this week with the people in Zambia will also become powerful encounters with the Savior.

Don't underestimate your impact. People will be overwhelmed when you decide to step out in faith and join the fight against extreme poverty.

He is calling each one of us to step out of our comfort zones and to touch the untouchables that we encounter on a regular basis.

Please pray, *"O Lord, use me as your hands to touch the lives of those who suffer. Here I am, send me!"* Amen.

Sunday

Our Last Day In Lusaka

I t's Sunday and we can't believe it's our final day in Zambia. We wake up, have breakfast and meet Esther in the lobby. Today, instead of doing a daily devotional from Pastor Andy, we head off to a local church for a morning service.

Zambia. We wake up, have breakfast and meet Esther in the lobby. Today, instead of doing a daily devotional from Pastor Andy, we head off to a local church for a morning service.

Zambian Church: We spend the morning visiting a Zambian church. We're surprised at all the nice cars in the parking lot. We are greeted warmly as we enter, and people ask us what we are in town to do. We tell them all about our work at Needs Care in Ngombe Compound. They are surprised to hear it.

It's a beautiful service and a beautiful place. During the service, we try to apply the sermon to all that we've seen and learned this week. We struggle to piece it all together, so we quietly pray,

> *"God, help me understand what I've seen here this week. Help me have your heart for the poor, the orphans, and widows. Help me live out my faith in authentic ways."*

We ask them if they have any programs or outreach activities in Ngombe, but they say "No." They have programs at their church, and in a nearby neighborhood, but not in Ngombe.

Tourist Market: After church, we visit the tourist market, browse the fun stalls, and look at all the handmade items. We eat a nice meal at a nearby restaurant and then return for more shopping. All too quickly, the afternoon is over.

Departure For The Hotel: Back at the hotel, we get cleaned up, head off to dinner, return early to pack; and then all too quickly, day seven is done. The next morning we head to the airport and begin our long journey home.

PART SIX

Partner Resources

"Your work is going to fill a large part of your life,
and the only way to be truly satisfied is to do what you
believe is great work. And the only way to do great work is to love
what you do. If you haven't found it yet, keep looking. Don't settle.
As with all matters of the heart, you'll know it when you find it."

—Steve Jobs

Help Wanted

By Jason

W e'd like to invite you to join our team and become a regional coordinator for Sew Powerful. It's official—you're hired! The job is simple—be our ambassador in your community and spread the word about Sew Powerful as vibrantly as you can.

This is a volunteer position; you get to define your own hours, and determine how you approach your work. In this chapter, we'll try to help with messaging, and outline a list of activities that you can choose from. You can do some of them, or all of them, depending on your personal situation. It's up to you. To get resources, our personal help, and let us know you've decided to become our regional coordinator, join our private group:

https://www.facebook.com/groups/
sewpowerfulregionalcoordinators/

Super Volunteer: Not ready to be a regional coordinator, but still super passionate about helping Sew Powerful? That's great too. We'd love for you to consider the ideas in this chapter your to-do list. Each one that you can complete is tremendously helpful. It might not seem like a big deal, but every action you take to help us is a godsend to the women and children of Zambia.

How To Share The Sew Powerful Story

We frequently ask people how they heard about Sew Powerful. The most common answer is, *"Somebody shared about it in my group."* So our strongest recommendation is that you re-read this book, and pick out the major aspects of Sew Powerful that you think are vital—and share them in your own way. In our view, the major highlights could include:

✓ Sew Powerful is a charity organization combating extreme poverty in Zambia through sewing.

✓ They employ seamstresses in Ngombe (pronounced Nom-bay), an incredibly desperate slum in the capital city of Lusaka.

✓ The seamstresses are paid for their work, which transforms their lives; but they also focus on making Purposeful Products, which are essential items to help the children of the community stay in school. They make two things: school uniforms and a reusable feminine hygiene product.

✓ Sixty percent of the children they work with are HIV Positive, and 2/3rds are orphans.

✓ Poor girls stay home from school when they are on their period, because they can't afford any products.

✓ On average these girls miss six weeks of school and fail to enter high school at a higher rate than boys.

✓ Reusable products are the best solution, because they last so long; and because in slums, and even in rural villages, disposable products create an ecological disaster.

✓ According to the U.N., when a teen girl fails to complete high school (called Secondary School there), she is four times more likely to contract HIV, will have a 40% higher pregnancy rate, and is seven times more likely to have a teenage marriage.

✓ Helping is easy! The Sew Powerful Purse program allows seamstresses from around the world to sew beautiful cross body purses, and send them in. Then the seamstresses in Zambia place the reusable feminine hygiene supplies, soap, and underwear in the purses, and conduct health training with the students.

✓ The students even take a Sew Powerful Pledge to stay in school all month if they receive a purse.

✓ Sew Powerful is also working with the seamstresses to transform their community through education, child and community health, and food strategies. So, there are other ways to help too, if you don't sew.

Who To Share With

Now that you have the basic story down, here are ideas that you can easily replicate related to sharing the story. All of them are free or low cost. With each activity in this chapter that you complete, you help us tremendously. Sharing with different types of people might take slightly different strategies, but the basic message is the same.

Sharing With Seamstresses: From our point of view, the process of sharing about Sew Powerful is very different, depending on whether you're sharing with a seamstress or a non-seamstress. Our messaging, branding, and purse program generally click with seamstresses. You'll immediately recognize that. Speaking with your sewing friends about Sew Powerful will probably be your most casual and low-stress conversation. A simple statement will probably do, something like this: *"Have you heard about the Sew Powerful Purse project yet? Oh my gosh, you'll love this..."*

Sharing With Non-Seamstresses: We're doing our best to try to expand our story and marketing material to ensure that it's relevant to non-seamstresses as well. So in addition to the basic story outlined above, here are a few areas you might want to emphasize if you're talking to non-seamstresses.

✓ Sew Powerful is focused on providing skills training and jobs, rather than hand-outs, to the moms and grandmas of Ngombe Compound, a desperately poor slum in Lusaka, Zambia.

✓ The program employs them to make Purposeful Products, essential items that the children in the community need to go to, and stay in school—specifically, uniforms and reusable feminine hygiene product.

✓ The community members help pay the seamstresses too. The parents or guardians pay in micro-installments for the school uniforms.

✓ The seamstresses are working hard to transform their community—to improve the local school and help feed the local children.

✓ Because many of the children they work with are HIV Positive, and desperately need food to stay on their Anti-Retroviral (ARV) drugs, they even have a farm dedicated to feeding the local kids.

✓ The farm employs people too, and it's 100% dedicated to feeding the children in Ngombe.

✓ Sew Powerful was started by small business owners Jason and Cinnamon Miles, so they have a passion for job creation and product marketing—not handouts.

Presentation And Sharing Tools:

We are working hard to create sharing tools. Check our Regional Coordinator Facebook group often, because we might have new things available that you're not aware of. If we don't have something, you can recommend it. The list currently includes:

Help Wanted

The Sew Powerful Cross Body Purse Pattern: Obviously, this is our signature tool for connecting with seamstresses. It's prominently featured on our website homepage. You can simply send people to the website to learn more. We collect the email address of each person that downloads the pattern, and then add him or her to our weekly newsletter; so it's important that you emphasize getting the pattern from our homepage. There is also a sew-along video, which is very helpful for seamstresses.

*The **We Are Sew Powerful** Book:* We hope you consider this book your best sharing tool, particularly for non-seamstresses. We'd love to have you act like Johnny Appleseed and share it widely across your community. Getting this book into the hands of as many people as possible is our primary marketing goal. Unfortunately, we can't give copies for free, but we can offer you multipacks at deep discounts on our website. It's important to remember that all the proceeds of this book go directly to supporting the Sew Powerful programs—so as you purchase it, you help grow the program. You can see all the details about the book on

http://www.sewpowerful.org/we-are-sew-powerful-book

The Sew Powerful Parables: As you're about to learn in an upcoming chapter, we are passionate about offering Sew Powerful parables as a resource for families, schools, and churches. We think they'll be particularly helpful to pastors. You can share individual parables, or share about them in general. See what we have at

http://www.sewpowerful.org/parables

Videos and PowerPoint Presentations: We are working hard to create more and better videos that tell our story. Be sure to check to see what we have on

http://www.sewpowerful.org/videos

Flyers and Posters: As with videos and presentations, we are working hard to create more and better flyers. Be sure to check to see what we have on:

http://sewpowerful.org/flyers

Specific People To Contact

We'd love to have you reach out beyond your circle of immediate friends. Here is a list of people to contact, with our recommendations on how to approach them. Clearly, these are harder conversations; but your number one asset is your passion for the program. Appeal to people's generosity, their desire to back smart strategies, and of course, strive to create win-win situations. Always remember, people are mentally tuned to the station, WIIFM (what's-in-it-for-me), so be sure you have an answer to that frequently unspoken question.

Bookstores In Your Community: Local bookstores in your area are excellent places to approach formally. This would be our #1 request. Ask to speak with a manager. Ask them to consider carrying *We Are Sew Powerful* on their bookshelves or front counter. It is already an Amazon #1 Bestseller in the Charity and Philanthropy category. If you're able to purchase a few, you could even offer to give them several free copies that they can sell—to see if their customers are interested.

Sewing and Fabric Stores: Take the same approach with a sewing or fabric store that you would with a local bookstore. In sewing stores, offer to coordinate a purse sewing class for charity for free. Of course, if nothing else, these locations also have community bulletin boards for flyers.

Church Mission Committees and Pastors: Consider approaching each church in your community and ask if they have a sewing group you can chat with. If you can meet with a church missions committee, or pastoral staff, that's even better. At a minimum, if you attend a church, then mention the book and parables to your pastors. Explain your enthusiasm and ask how the church can get involved.

>

One question churches have asked us is *"How is this tied to preaching the Gospel?"* Our answer is simple. 85% of the people in Zambia are Christians, so our emphasis is on helping the orphans and widows in their time of need (see James 1:27). We do that in partnership with Christian ministries, and they focus on the evangelism so that we can focus on employment of women to empower the education of orphans.

School and Community Leaders: School librarians, teachers, and various types of community leaders will find this book and the Sew Powerful Parables particularly helpful. So consider approaching them with a *"recommendation for helpful resources."*

Business And Corporate Leaders: We realize that our Christian worldview and ministry mindedness might feel too religious for a lot of companies—but not all of them. When approaching these types of leaders, it's probably wise to underscore this sentence,

> *"We focus on employment for women to*
> *empower the education of orphans."*

That is a message most leaders could enthusiastically support. It puts us in the same category as many faith-based charities that have massive corporate support, including Habitat For Humanity and others.

If you have strong contacts with local business owners or senior leaders, then approach them personally and ask if their company would ever consider being involved. If by chance you know people at sewing or fashion-related companies—all the better. If you happen to know someone at Kate Spade, Michael Kors, or Hermes, then by all means approach them. We would love to be the "charity of choice" for the fashion and handbag industry. Imagine how powerful that would be!

The Christmas and Birthday Gift Strategy

An easy way to spread the word with your family is to give We Are Sew Powerful as a Christmas gift as widely as possible. Again, multipacks are available at a deep discount on our website. Tell them it was your favorite book of the year, and that they will love it, regardless of whether they sew or not.

Or turn this strategy around and ask your family members to buy you a copy of *We Are Sew Powerful* as your Christmas or birthday gift. Ask them all to buy you a copy. Explain to them that since you don't need anything, you want a lot of copies because you are going to re-gift all of the copies you get to local friends and business owners as part of your Regional Coordinator duties for Sew Powerful.

How To Include People

Ask People To Help: If you sew, then expand your process to include a few people. Throw a party and invite them to help you make purses. If they don't sew, they can cut, iron, write note cards, etc. If they don't sew and want to learn, offer to teach them. Each time you slow down and include people in your process, you expand your local team.

Ask For a Formal Blessing: Not long ago we saw an amazing picture of Sew Powerful purses on the altar of a church. So we asked the person who posted it, Vivian Bigley Sylvester, to share more about the story. She explained a very creative engagement strategy that we think any of you could copy. You might not be invited to speak at your church, but your minister might take the time to do a formal blessing of the purses during a service. That would be amazing! Here is what she said,

> We are getting ready to send out our first batch of purses (45 total) and decided to take them to the church for a blessing before they start their journey. I spoke about the project, and our pastor led the congregation in prayers for the ministry and the girls who will receive the purses. Many in the congregation hadn't seen the purses before and were very enthusiastic about the project. We never could have imagined how successful this project has become for us, and we are energized to keep going. THANK YOU for starting such a wonderful program to empower the schoolgirls to continue their education and improve their lives.

Ask For Note Card Writers: As Kevin LaRoche will share in his upcoming chapter, young people would be happy to write note cards for your purses. Many people in your community probably would be. This gives you the opportunity to share about the program, explain the need, and get people involved.

Coordinate A Larger Sewing Event: Follow the details in Terah Lites' upcoming chapter about putting on a sewing event. Or if you feel like that is not in your skillset, then begin networking with people until you find a project coordinator that has the skill and enthusiasm to help you make it a reality. You can serve as the sewing coach.

Help Us On Amazon: Leaving this book a positive review on Amazon is a massive help. Amazon shows books with a large number of reviews to a broader audience. We'd appreciate your highest and best review as a way to help spread the word.

Conclusion: We live in a new era. The world is smaller and more connected than it ever has been before. You are one email, one conversation, one presentation away from dramatically improving the lives of the women and children of Ngombe.

In the past you might have felt like you couldn't make a difference from your home. But you really can. You can help us radically improve the lives of people in Zambia. We hope you'll strongly consider joining us in sharing the message.

Youth Leader Resources

By Kevin LaRoche

Wildfire Student Ministry, Renton Washington

*A*s a Youth Pastor and Sew Powerful board member, I've been praying and thinking about how to engage my young people in the work of Sew Powerful for several years. I am always looking for ways to help students shine bright and make a difference in their world. I don't have it all figured out, but here are several ideas you might want to explore that will help your group and Sew Powerful.

Aspiring Fashion Stars

If you have a group of purse makers at your church, then try to ensure that they invite the teens to get involved, especially if there is a group event. If just one teen girl gets a vision for helping—she'll bring others.

Fashion and design is incredibly trendy these days—hasn't it always been? Girls interested in fashion design need to learn how to sew, and having someone show them is a terrific way to help them and build a relationship. Using the Sew Powerful Purse program to deepen the connections in your church between young and old is a fantastic idea.

Note Card Writing

Our teens were happy to participate in the 2015 unboxing party and looking forward to doing it again in the future. That's easy for us because we are local.

But there were so many purses that showed up that didn't have note cards and needed them. It was a perfect activity for the young people. They loved it. Once they understood the program, they were eager to have the opportunity to encourage someone else in a desperate situation. They did a great job. If you have teenagers in your church and you need note cards written for purses you make, ask them to help you!

3 Meals Matter™ Fundraising Event

When the 3 Esthers Farm program started, I began thinking about past fundraisers we had done that were focused on feeding hungry children. We began to wonder if we could conduct an overnight event as a fundraiser so our teens could help raise money for the farm. See what we've done and get the tools we used on:

http://www.3esthersfarm.org

Here is an overview of the **3 Meals Matter™** Program we've created, and are launching in the fall of 2016. We'd love to have you replicate our model and help us make the 3 Esthers Farm a powerhouse of food production in support of the starving kids at the Needs Care School.

Program Overview: An annual youth group fundraising event to support feeding hungry children via the 3 Esthers Farm. Teens pledge to skip three meals and ask other people to sponsor them as they do it.

Program Name: *3 Meals Matter™*

Program Duration and Milestones: We've found that launching your program six to eight weeks prior to your culminating event is a good timeframe to consider. The distinct phases are:

Campaign Kick-Off: Announce the campaign to your group and explain the desperate situation of the children at the Needs Care School. Rally them to support the project.

Fundraising Phase: Update the teens each week throughout the fundraising phase, and share praise reports, funny stories, and general encouragement. Create incentives and prizes to motivate their hard work.

Final Event: Plan a fun final event where you skip the three meals together, and then celebrate with a large party to complete the project. The final event can take many forms; our preferred method is an over-nighter, where we program specific fun activities, service projects, as well as Bible studies.

Bible Study Topics: There are lots of related topics that could be used during the campaign. Self sacrifice, caring for orphans, personal discipline, and God's calling on our lives to serve others are just a few. We are going to work to have a set of devotionals written by Andy Smith in support of our event. We're happy to make them available for your use.

Program Materials: We are working hard to create fundraising materials for our inaugural event and we're happy to make them available to you as well. Get them at:

http://www.3esthersfarm.org

Fundraising/Donor Giving Tools: The Sew Powerful team has set up online fundraising tools via the Crowdrise Platform to make it easy for us. Learn how to access them at:

http://www.3esthersfarm.org

Join Us

We'd love to be a resource for you as you develop strategies to get your youth group involved; and if you conduct a 3 Meals Matter™ event, please let us know. Maybe the materials and strategies you create can be shared with others via the Sew Powerful Newsletter.

Sew Powerful Parables

By Dana Buck

I am so proud to be a board member here at Sew Powerful. I'm constantly amazed and impressed with what we're able to do to touch the lives of girls and women in Zambia through Sew Powerful, and I'm always looking for ways to get more involved.

But here's a little secret—I don't know how to sew. But I do know how to write, so I took the liberty of putting together a little story several months back called Royal Blue with Stripes of Red. I hoped it would capture some of the magic and impact of what we do through Sew Powerful and the Sew Powerful Purse. I was shocked when it had more than 10,000 views on Facebook in the first few weeks. You can see it at:

http://www.sewpowerful.org/parables/

But, as with most things, the journey has been every bit as important as the destination. If you'll indulge me, here is my story.

My journey to writing what I feel are God-inspired parables for families and churches has been one of being "sweetly broken" and "gently rebuilt" under the hand of a loving God. First, some background. I've been a Christian since I was 18 years old. I've served in leadership positions for one of the largest Christian organizations in the country for over 37 years.

I've brought the word of God to large audiences at events all around the country. I've been a leader in my church, and spoken from the pulpit dozens of times. I'm a husband, father, brother, son, colleague and friend. And, I am deeply flawed and in desperate need of a Savior. You see, all the accomplishments, responsibilities, accolades, success, etc., can create a subtle yet unhealthy opportunity for ego and self to intrude where God alone should reign and be praised.

The problem is that it all looks really good from the outside. It looks like service; it looks like sacrifice—it looks honorable. It can fool those looking in from the outside. And, it can fool you too. Does any of this sound familiar?

God wanted to do a new thing in me and through me, but he couldn't do it on the foundation I had built. Don't get me wrong, I never walked away from Christ. I never lost my desire to serve him and honor him. But what I did lose was the self-awareness and self-honesty to see that, although I never stopped standing on the firm foundation of the Rock, I was certainly good at building little add-on annexes that looked good, looked like the Rock, but were, in truth, a fragile veneer of spirituality that covered the unstable sand of self and ego. God loved me too much to allow that to continue.

So, in September of 2015, I found myself in an emergency hospital room after an emotional breakdown. I didn't know what was happening to me. Was I having a stroke? A heart attack? It turns out nothing was physically wrong, and I was sent home with the advice to see my doctor and seek counseling from someone who could help me understand what had happened and why. This episode happened at work in front of dozens of my colleagues. Family and friends soon learned what had occurred.

The myth that I was strong, confident, capable, in control, etc., was shattered. The foundation of my image of myself, and the image I projected to others was gone in an instant. What remained was confusion, vulnerability, fear and brokenness. God had me right where he wanted me.

As I sat on the edge of my bed after waking from 26 hours of sleep, in a moment of extreme clarity I asked no one in particular *"What happened to me?"* In that moment I felt God's touch and presence in a way I rarely have before. He put his arms around me and said, *"I'm raising up a testimony in you."* Out loud I replied, *"I don't want it, thank you very much."*

In my mind I was immediately taken to John, chapter 6, in which Jesus begins to tell the multitudes the cost of being his disciple. In response, almost all walk away from him. He turns to his twelve chosen disciples and says *"What about you, will you leave also?"* Peter (good old Peter) says, *"Where would we go?"* I knew that there was nowhere to turn but to the one I had committed to follow. I told the Lord that whatever he had to teach me and whatever he was about, I would follow. God gave me three thoughts as I sat there; *"Don't be afraid, trust in me, see it through."* I had no idea what "it" was, but just like Peter I said, *"Where else can I go?"*

Through the weeks and months that followed, I found myself on leave from work. I built a relationship with a Christian counselor who helped me see what God was doing and identify the areas in my life that needed His attention. My counselor called it "pruning." I call it a difficult process of examination and honesty, which, although hard, allowed God to chip away the dross from the foundation of my life and bring it back to solid Rock. It's a process that is and will be on going until he calls me home.

My pastor, who has been a great support through this journey, asked me if I'd be willing to share in church my experiences and learnings with the congregation. I had some trepidation but, from the beginning I felt that, if indeed God was raising up a testimony in me, I needed to be honest and willing to be open to share what had happened to me. So, I said yes.

In preparation for that, I was reading in Romans 7 and 8 about the struggle of the two natures inside us all – the one that seeks to please God, and the other that seeks to please the flesh. It was in this context that I decided to share my story. So, one morning, about a week before Christmas, I was home wrapping Christmas presents. I had a hot cup of coffee, the house was peaceful and quiet, and I had the station on my cell phone tuned to a holiday channel. Suddenly what came on was "How the Grinch Stole Christmas" by Dr. Seuss—not just the song, but the entire book, read by none other than Boris Karloff. I had loved this story ever since I was a boy, and I can't tell you how cool it was to wrap gifts, drink coffee and enjoy that story.

When it was done, I thought to myself *"What a cool way to communicate the spirit of Christmas in a way that is charming for kids, but also speaks to an adult."* Once again I felt the arms of the Lord encompass me and say in my heart *"I created you to do that."* Well that was out of the blue.

All my life I had written little rhyming poems and stories for people's birthdays, holiday parties, as well as for my wife when I was courting her. (It must have worked!) So, I set out to illustrate the battle of the two natures through a rhyming story called *Rickett & Shine*, two dogs who live in a man's backyard and represent those two natures. The moral of the story: whichever dog you feed will be the stronger dog.

I spoke in church and presented that story to a wonderful reception and encouragement from the congregation. Through that experience, I began to see that a gift God had given me, that I had treated rather frivolously, could be used to great effect when offered back to him. I started to understand the new thing God wanted to do in me and through me, and why that couldn't happen without cleaning up the foundation first.

Now, almost a year later, I have 18 completed "parables," with number 19 in process in my notebook as we speak. I have had the opportunity to share these stories (and my personal testimony) with hundreds of people, and have enjoyed the aftermath of questions, comments and personal stories shared by those who were touched by what I've written and what I've shared about my own experience. God has taken brokenness and confusion and turned it into an opportunity to share his goodness. What an amazing God we serve!

As we worked on the Royal Blue video together, I asked Jason and Cinnamon if they thought these parables could be useful to Sew Powerful; they said, *"Absolutely!"* So the "Sew Powerful Parables" are offered as a gift from us at Sew Powerful to all who want to hear and share the encouragement of the Lord in a fun and unique way. We'll continue to add them, make videos, and even include devotional guides written by Andy Smith. See what we have at:

www.sewpowerful.org/parables/

We are all on a journey, and our experiences and learnings can serve as a road map for those who are walking the same path. Our lives are a testimony in the making in the hands of a loving God. May it always be so!

Here is *Royal Blue With Stripes Of Red:*

> In a humble sewing room
> Among the pins and thread
> Lay a little piece of fabric
> Royal blue with stripes of red.
>
> It was a piece left over
> From a project done in May;
> It fell outside the pattern
> So was neatly cut away.
>
> Set aside now and forgotten
> It lay while pants and skirts
> Were made in great profusion
> Along with shorts and shirts.
>
> So the dust began to settle
> As the weeks went by and by,
> And this little piece of fabric
> Could not catch the seamstress' eye.

Then one day the room was filled
With laughter and with light;
The seamstress seemed so happy
Yes, her mood was sheer delight!

And as she settled down to work
Her machine was quickly humming
And soon a strap and bag with flap
Was quickly up and coming.

When her project seemed completed
One detail seemed to block it
She raised her head, "I know," she said
"It needs a little pocket!"

She searched among her fabrics
Through the muted and the bright
Although she'd many options
Nothing struck her as just right.

Was then that something caught her eye
And as she turned her head
She spied the perfect piece of cloth
Royal blue with stripes of red.

She set herself to sewing
And her needle swiftly played
Soon she stopped and smiled upon
The purse that she had made.

And in the special pocket
She gently tucked a note
She'd prayed softly as she'd penned it
And here is what she wrote.

"This little purse is special
It's for a friend I'll never meet,
Made with love and filled with joy
For a girl who's young and sweet."

"So I give it as an offering
As God would have me do
I close my eyes and see your face
For my dear, that friend is you!"

The purse was wrapped and readied
And then dropped into the mail
To begin a magic journey
And to start a brand new tale.

For after epic travel
And when finally it arrived
Caring hands prepared it
And placed special things inside.

It's then, this gift is ready
Coming halfway round the world
To be placed into the waiting hands
Of a bright and lovely girl.

She loved it from the very start
To her it's like a jewel
The contents help to keep her clean
And also stay in school.

The thing she loves above all else
That makes her spirit float,
Words from a friend she'll never meet
Written in a note.

We Are Sew Powerful

After reading for the hundredth time
The note and what it said,
She tucks it in the pocket
Royal blue with stripes of red.

Sewing Event Resources

Terah Lites

*S*ew Powerful has caught your eye. Maybe it was on Instagram; maybe it was through Facebook or the website, or maybe it was just word of mouth. In the end, it doesn't really matter how you got here, we are just glad you did.

The more people we have who are excited about this project, the greater our impact will be. So, you have the pattern, you've even made a purse, but you are still wondering, *"What else can I do? I can only make so many purses."*

Well, guess what? There is an answer: Host an event! I did just that, and it was an *awesome* experience! I want to share that experience with you and give you some practical tips, which will help your Sew Powerful event be a success. Find all the resources mentioned in this chapter at:

http://sewpowerful.org/event-resources/

A Sew Powerful Event can be done in a myriad of ways, but in this chapter I will lay out some of the basic ideas to help you get started. From there, you can run with it and make it your own!

Simply put, a Sew Powerful Event is when people, who are willing and passionate about making a difference in the lives of others, gather together and use their sewing skills to do just that.

Location

The first thing to consider is where your event will take place. There are a couple of important things to keep in mind as you think about your location.

Space: Sewing takes up space. When several people are gathering to sew, make sure there is adequate space to do so. You will need room and tables for cutting, places to set up sewing machines, and room for irons and ironing boards. You might even have a fabric donation area that will need to be sorted, as well.

Electricity: If your event is small, this shouldn't be a problem; but if you are meeting at a large location, you want to keep in mind how many machines and irons you will need to plug in, and prepare accordingly with power strips and extension cords.

We held our event in the Fellowship Hall at my church. This worked great for us! Some other ideas might be:

Someone's House: Different stations could be set up in different rooms.

A Community Building: Sometimes you can rent out space in your community. A lot of times, if you tell them what you are doing, they might even donate the space for free.

Sewing/Crafting Shops: There might already be shops or studios in your area that would love to get involved in a project like this. It never hurts to ask! I have found that most of the time, when people find out what you are doing, they can't wait to help out.

Basically, where there's a will, there's a way. Just find a location, pick a date and get started!

Preliminary Planning

Once you have a location, you are ready to get started with the planning. I would plan on three hours minimum for a good, productive event.

That's about how long it takes to make one purse from cut to finish for the average seamstress.

Now you are ready to publicize! We announced it in our church bulletin, created an event on Facebook, and announced it on Instagram. We had a total of nine women cutting and sewing purses. Ours was small but worked really well for the time and space we had available.

Make sure to have people RSVP, so you can plan accordingly. We had two different sewing/ironing stations and one area to sort fabric.

One pretty cool thing that happened with our event is that a local sewing store, Calico Corners, donated two large bags of fabric. One of the ladies who was attending the event decided to go in there the day before and ask if they would be interested in donating any remnants; they were more than happy to donate, once they learned about our cause. Don't be afraid to ask! Compassionate people are everywhere just waiting to pitch in.

If you have a limited amount of time, another thing that might be helpful is to cut out sets of purses ahead of time. I created a "Pattern Label" document for this. That way you only need one pattern to reuse over and over. Just remove the pattern piece after cutting and pin the corresponding label on the cut piece.

This document, along with pictures of our event can be found on the Sew Powerful website at:

http://sewpowerful.org/event-resources/

Once we had the purse sets cut out, we kept them in gallon-sized plastic bags to keep them organized.

What to Bring

As we were inviting people to the event, we realized that we needed a good list of what they would need to bring.

First of all, whether they are sewing or not, I would direct them to the Sew Powerful website and have them download the pattern.

This will not only give them a chance to cut when they arrive, but it will also offer opportunity to explore more about what Sew Powerful does and sign up to receive updates. They could even start to cut out purses ahead of time. If they are sewing, then they will need to bring the following:

Sewing machine: Don't forget the power cord! I actually did this, and my husband and a friend came to the rescue!

Sewing supplies: Scissors, seam ripper, pins, choice of fabrics, a printed pattern

Irons: You will also need people to bring irons and ironing boards. We found that we didn't each need our own. If you have one to share between two or three people, that worked well for us.

If they are only cutting, then all they will need are the pattern and a good pair of fabric cutting scissors. If they are writing postcards, they can just bring themselves!

Event Set Up

I created this checklist as we planned and hosted the event. It will make it much easier for me to host a second event, and can also be used by anyone who would like to host their own.

- ✓ Location:
- ✓ Time and Day:
- ✓ Number of people:
- ✓ Tables needed:
- ✓ Electrical outlets, power strips, or extension cords needed:
- ✓ Number of sewing machines/stations:
- ✓ Number of irons:
- ✓ Number of cutting stations:
- ✓ Will there be a fabric sorting area:
- ✓ Note card writing table with supplies:

Keep this checklist with you when you are prepping for the event. If you are able to get into your location the day before, you can get most of it set up and ready to go early.

If you only have access the day of the event, then allow a couple of hours before your event to set up. Also, don't think you have to do all of this alone. People love to help when they know they are needed. All you have to do is ask. We actually had a group of middle school girls meeting at our church the night before our event, so when they were done, they were able to set up our tables for us. It was a huge help and they loved doing it!

Because this turned out to be an all-women's event for us, we recruited some of the men in our church to be the ones to provide some light refreshments. This was my co-host's idea, and I thought it was a great one. We just had some fruit, muffins, and coffee, but what a great idea for getting the men involved as well!

One other very important aspect of your event is to document it. Sew Powerful is always looking for great stories about how this program is impacting lives, not only in Africa, but all over the world. If you share on social media, use the hashtags:

#sewpowerfulpurse

#sewpowerful

#wearesewpowerful

If you don't know what that last suggestion means, ask a teenager to help you. They'll explain it and can help you share your pictures with the world.

I have a close friend who just so happens to be an amazing photographer, so I asked her to come and photograph our event for us. We had a lot of fun with this, and I'm sure you will, too!

Even if you don't have a professional photographer in your midst, take pictures anyway. Write down who was there and document any meaningful stories that you want to remember from the day.

Note Cards

The last thing on the checklist is note card writing. This is such a crucial part of the process. Each purse that is given in Africa will contain one of these note cards. We cannot even imagine what it must be like to not have someone care enough about you to speak truth and love into your life. That is what these note cards do. They let the girls know that someone in the world cares about them and even more so, that God cares about them. They also help you to remember why it is you are doing this in the first place.

Many of these girls are orphans. Many do not have food on a regular basis. And many are even the head of their household. These girls have tough lives, and by sewing a purse and including some heartfelt words, you are making a difference. It might be the difference that could change the course of her life. Make sure you do not skip the note cards!

Before we had our event, Jason gave me the idea of having some themes in case people were having trouble thinking of something to say. This was really helpful to our ladies. Themes like:

- ✓ You're not alone…
- ✓ God is a good father…
- ✓ We believe in you…
- ✓ Study hard; you can do it…
- ✓ God will make a way…
- ✓ Jesus loves you…
- ✓ God has a plan…
- ✓ God has a purpose for your life…
- ✓ God has good things in store for you…
- ✓ Never give up…
- ✓ Stay in school…

I didn't have time before our event, but I thought it would be really nice to print up posters of some of these themes and have them on the wall above a table with the blank postcards and some writing supplies.

Another great thing to know is that Sew Powerful is always getting more purses than note cards. So, if you have someone coming to your event that is not a big sewer, maybe that person would like to write note cards the whole time. Just send in your extra notes with the purses, and the Sew Powerful staff and volunteers will distribute them where they are needed.

The Day of the Event

The first thing we did on the day of our event was open with prayer. It is easy to get bogged down with details and forget why you are there, so we took a minute to quiet our minds and thank God that we get to be a part of someone's story. It was a sweet time.

I then took some time to introduce Sew Powerful. Some of the ladies were invited by word of mouth, and did not know the backstory of Sew Powerful or that the co-founder, Cinnamon Miles, is my sister.

This was an especially meaningful time for me because I had a chance to share my heart for this ministry and these girls in a more in-depth way.

Once the ladies understood what we were doing and why, it energized them.

One of them, who is a retired journalist, offered to write up a piece covering our event and submit it to the local paper. You never know who is listening or how Sew Powerful's story is going to impact participants, so be sure to share it.

Next, take some time to point out the different stations, and if sewing machines still need to be set up, just assist wherever you are needed.

Again, you should have the following stations:

✓ Sewing Machines

✓ Cutting Area

- ✓ Fabric Sorting Area
- ✓ Note Card Writing Table
- ✓ Refreshments

Once everyone has a job and feels comfortable with what they are doing, just stand back for a minute and take it all in. It was a humbling experience for me, partly because this all started with my own sister and her husband.

As I stood there I started thinking about the girls in Zambia—the ones whose lives will be forever changed—all because a few people took some time out of their Saturday morning, and decided they wanted to make a difference.

People want to see lives eternally impacted and to make a difference. Your job is to explain to them that they can do just that, with a willing heart and a sewing machine.

Unseen Angels

By Jason

*I*f you'd like to join us financially, we've got several easy ways you can do that. Together we can show deep care and respect for the women and children of Ngombe Compound—and maybe all of Zambia.

Our *Atelier Angels* Program is a monthly pledge program of $9, $19, or $29, and the proceeds help ensure the sewing program thrives. Atelier (pronounced A-tal-ia) means "workshop" or "workroom." We truly believe we can serve as Angels (or maybe Angel Investors) to support the sewing cooperative.

You can join us right now by visiting:

http://www.sewpowerful.org/donate

Our Equation Includes You

The math involved is fairly simple. But it's not just about financial giving. It's about time, talent, and treasure too. We could even write it as an equation:

$$S + P + F = LCF$$

S   stands for *Seamstresses in Ngombe* making items at the sewing cooperative.

P stands for *Purse makers* around the world assisting the cooperative with beautiful purses.

F stands for Funding to cover the cost of delivering the purses to girls and expanding the program.

LCF stands for *Lives Changed Forever.* The lives include the children of Zambia, the Zambian seamstresses and their families, and the purse makers around the world.

Why We Need Your Help So Urgently

Our overall program is constrained in Ngombe for several reasons. If we are going to grow, it is going to take financial investment.

We have two locations that we are currently focused on expanding through donor giving: first, the sewing cooperative; and second, the 3 Esthers Farm. Here are more details about how financial giving can support each one.

Sewing Cooperative: The sewing cooperative is the heart of our effort. It offers employment—and the more people we can employ, the larger our impact can be on the community and all of Zambia. For that to occur, we need to overcome several obstacles including,

Space: The Needs Care School is gifting the current facility we use for our sewing room. If we are going to grow the program to reach more children, the sewing cooperative in Ngombe needs its own expanded space that is designed for large-scale sewing production work. Additionally, the school is bursting at the seams, so they could really use the room for their other programs.

Machines: We need more and better sewing machines that are dependable and that can handle constant daily use. We can't grow the number of seamstresses unless we also grow the number of machines. Unfortunately, we can't accept random donations of one-off machines because we've found that it's vital to have most, if not all of the seamstresses using the same machine, so they can cross-train and quickly resolve repair issues.

Seamstresses: There are hundreds of women in Ngombe that would gladly join us, and would be thrilled to have a sewing job that is tied to such important educational achievement goals. To employ them, we need funds for salary dollars.

3 Esthers Farm: The farm has the potential to meet the food needs of the children of Needs Care. But it's just getting started, and we have a lot of work to do. To give financially to the farm visit:

http://3esthersfarm.org/give-today/

As we mentioned in a prior chapter, we need to do a series of infrastructure projects including:

- ✓ Electricity being run to the farm by the regional utility company
- ✓ Wiring the Caretaker's house
- ✓ Acquiring all the equipment needed to transform our hand-pumped well into a complete watering system; including a metal tower, large water tank, electric water pump, and all the pipes and hoses to enable a better watering system
- ✓ A barn for a large chicken project
- ✓ More farm hands to expand production
- ✓ A vehicle for hauling items

More Than Just Food

The farm also has the opportunity to employ people in support of the important goal of feeding the children of Needs Care. Each person we can employ is earning an income that changes the story of their family. They are investing their time and talent toward a noble purpose, and they get paid for doing good.

But the farm has more value than even employment. Most of the children of Ngombe haven't been too far outside Ngombe. Some may have traveled into Lusaka with their parents or guardians. Maybe some of traveled to distant villages to visit family, but those are very rare situations. The farm serves as a perfect place for field trips for the children. They can learn about animals, farming, science, and so much more.

General Support of The School

As our program grows, we hope to fund general support of the school more and more. This includes things like teacher salaries, supplies, support staff, maintenance, facility expansion, and the school clinic program.

The Power of $5

We've designed the Sew Powerful Purse program so that for just $4.93 we can deliver a purse with all the items inside.

At the 3 Esthers Farm we can plant an orange tree for less than $5 that will produce 3,000 oranges a year when mature.

Less than $5 really can change someone's life.

In the case of the purse program, a small financial gift can help provide employment to a seamstress, enable educational achievement at a critical time, provide dignity, and demonstrate that you care.

In the case of the 3 Esthers Farm, an orange tree can help provide employment to a farm hand, enable a child to have good overall nutrition, stay focused in school, and even help them keep their Anti-Retroviral medication down—potentially saving their lives.

Please don't underestimate the impact of even a small financial gift.

We'd welcome your partnership. You can give via debit card, credit card or PayPal at:

http://sewpowerful.org/donate/

To give via check simply make it out to:

Sew Powerful
218 E. Main Street
Auburn, WA 98002

Conclusion

By Jason

W e are incredibly honored that you've taken the time to learn our story, the story of the seamstresses, the stories of our amazing donors and partners, and most importantly the story of the children of the Needs Care School.

But the story is just getting started. In a few years we'll need to revise and expand this book because of all the amazing things that have yet to occur. We hope you'll decide to join us and help make them happen. Together we really are Sew Powerful.

To find out the latest developments in our program be sure to visit us at

www.sewpowerful.org

Jason & Cinnamon Miles

Auburn, WA

Notes

Unless otherwise cited, we gathered the statistics for this book from United Nations documents. To learn more about these topics we'd encourage you to read the following:

http://www.uis.unesco.org/Education/Documents/
unesco-from-access-to-equality-2012.pdf

http://en.unesco.org/gem-report/sites/gem-report/
files/girls-factsheet-en.pdf

http://www.unicef.org/lifeskills/index_8657.html

http://www.unaids.org/sites/default/files/media_
asset/UNAIDS_HIV_prevention_among_adolescent_
girls_and_young_women.pdf

Made in the USA
Lexington, KY
01 June 2019